A Gift From
the Heart

A Gift From the Heart

ESPECIALLY
FOR MY CHILDREN

Mary E. Sayers

This book was printed in the United States of America.

To order additional copies of this book, contact:
Xlibris Corporation
1-888-795-4274
www.Xlibris.com
Orders@Xlibris.com
15625

Contents

DEDICATION

TO MY CHILDREN SO THEY CAN
BETTER UNDERSTAND ME
BECAUSE I LOVE THEM ALL SO DEARLY.

SHIRLEY ROSE—DECEASED
PATRICIA JOANN
WILLIAM JOHN
THOMAS JAMES
MICHAEL ANTHONY
CHRISTOPHER RAYMOND

Acknowledgments

S pecial thanks to my niece, Barb Lither, for helping type and edit my first draft. Due to the death of my husband Joseph and the loss of my vision to Macular Degeneration this book remained incomplete for the last three years. Then Dannie Sayers, my daughter in-law, came by and said, "Let's get this book published." Seven months later after many readings and editing we finally finished our task through much laughter and tears. Then my daughter in-law, Carol Sayers, sat on the floor sorting though hundreds of pictures for the book. Then my son, Michael, designed the cover, and edited the final chapters. The photo on the cover dipicts me at age five in front of our tar paper home in North Dakota. As kids growing up by the railroad tracks, the train engineers would delight us with a whistle blast and a wave. I got to relive that special memory a few years ago, on a return trip to the former homestead, hence photo number two. Forever gratitude to these four for putting the pressure on to get this book done. Without their help this book would never have been completed.

Many Thanks,

Mary Sayers

My Growing up Years

Beginnings

Mary Ernestine Patricia Winter	March 6, 1920 to November 25, 1990
French & Chippewa-Cree & German	

I was born the fifth of nine children in a family of two distinct cultures. My mother, Mama, was French and Indian, and my father a full-blooded German. Mama was a petite woman. She never weighed more than ninety five pounds and was four feet ten inches tall. My father was a strapping hulk of a man. He was six feet two inches tall. They were quite a contrast in both culture and size.

Mama's Parents—DesJarlais

Mary Ursula Martin	September 30, 1858 to March 20, 1939
French & Chippewa-Cree	
Andrew DesJarlais	1861 to May 17, 1943
French & Chippewa-Cree	

In 1893, Grandma and Grandpa DesJarlais, my mother's parents, traveled by wagon from Winnipeg, Canada, destination North Dakota, the southwestern part near the Montana border. They drove a team of horses and pulled a wagon that held all their worldly goods. They had a son three years old, and Grandma DesJarlais was quite pregnant. When they reached the middle of the state, Grandma went into labor. Grandpa stopped and set up a quick camp, none too soon, as my Mama made her appearance. That was the 31st day of May, 1893. The area was known as White Earth.

Andrew and Mary DesJarlais

After Grandma regained her strength, they continued on to Trenton, North Dakota. Their allotment of land had been issued to them by the

Bureau of Indian Affairs, and this would become their home. Grandpa DesJarlais's land in North Dakota was near the Montana border, where the Missouri River meets the Yellowstone River.

Mama

Mary Ernestine DesJarlais	May 31, 1893 to November 25, 1990
French & Chippewa-Cree	Married: August 31, 1912
Jack Peter Winter	May 14, 1882 to 1953
German & Chippewa-Cree	

Mama and her two brothers grew up and went to a public school. The name of the school was Painted Woods. Mama finished the eighth grade. At that time, it was equivalent to graduation from college. She was asked to teach, but she declined. She knew how she had been treated as an Indian student. In so short a time, how could things be any better?

Mama told us many stories about her childhood and her school days, and the adjustment she and all the other Indian kids had to make to fit into the white man's world. They were forbidden to speak their own language; if they were caught, they were beaten. They could not have long hair. It was easier to de-louse them with shorter hair.

As I am writing this, news is on the television. The date is December 2, 1996. They are expounding on the infestation of head lice in the public schools. In my mother's time and where I went to school, head lice would have been blamed solely on the Indians.

My mother and her two brothers also had a Bureau of Indian Affairs land allotment of one hundred sixty acres each. Her land was in Montana where she raised riding horses. Mama was an excellent horsewoman and was very proud of her horses.

Mama posing side saddle on her horse.

Mama Gets Married

In May of 1862, the US Congress passed the Homestead Act. It provided that any person over 21, who was the head of a family, and either a citizen or an alien who intended to become a citizen, could obtain the title to 160 acres of public land if they lived on the land for five years and improved it. Or, the settler could pay $1.25 an acre in place of the residence requirement. Although the Homestead Act was since modified, it is still in effect today.

The Homestead Act had opened up the Dakota Territory. My father and his five brothers came from Minnesota to start their own homesteads. They all filed for claims on adjoining properties.

The land my father's family settled on was my mother's allotted land. The Bureau of Indian Affairs just looked the other way.

Fort Buford was a very active fort, situated in Dakota Territory. In 1804, when the Lewis and Clark expedition went "that-a-way," this Fort had been an important outpost on the highway from St. Louis to the Rocky Mountains. The Fort was enlarged in 1867. The Commanding Officer bought old Fort Union just across the Montana border and used its timbers to enlarge Fort Buford.

After we came along, my brother and I used to play at the Fort. We would find the little round balls that the Army used in their guns. We used them in our sling shots. Today both forts are national monuments.

Mama worked in the trading post at Fort Buford. The trading post served Indians and the new settlers of "homesteaders." It seemed my father was out of supplies quite often.

So that is how my parents met. After a brief courtship, they were married. Both of their parents objected to this union. Dad truly had a gift of gab— how else could he have won the heart of so fair an Indian maiden? They were married in the Catholic Church at Trenton, North Dakota on August 31,

1912. Dad's parents were from Germany and Mama's parents were the "blue bloods of the prairie."

My father and mother's wedding picture (1912).

My Father's Parents— Winter

Catherine Dressell	February, 1849 to 1916
German	
Joseph Peter Winter	October, 1844 to unknown
German	

I did not know my German grandparents very well. They came from Minnesota to be near their sons. They had a farm in Medicine Lake, Montana and raised sheep, chickens, ducks and geese.

Their diet was so different from what we were used to. Grandma Winter made potato pancakes and other German dishes. Dad made all our sausage and he taught Mama how to make his favorite foods.

Grandpa and Grandma Winter had three daughters in addition to my father and his five brothers. That little lady gave birth to thirteen children, four of whom died. She raised six boys and three girls.

Grandmother Winter came to America from Germany when she was a young woman. Rumor has it that she was adopted at an early age. Her name was Catherine Dressell. She met Joseph Winter in a pub. He worked as a lumberjack in Minnesota and then started the pub. As I remember him, he was quite small in stature. Yet, as the story goes, when he saw this beautiful red-headed gal dancing on the bar, he boldly picked her up and made the statement, "She will dance no more as I intend to marry her." And this he did.

**My father's parents,
Joseph and Catherine Winter**

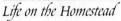
Life on the Homestead

Dad built a three room tar paper shack on his homestead. Mama's life was hard and lonely. She had sisters-in-law, but they, too, were very hateful with the exception of one of Dad's sisters, Aunt Louise. She was so kind to Mama and helped her a lot. We kids loved her so much. Her children were all about our ages, so we grew up together. Even when we moved back to the Dakotas, we never lost touch.

Mama had her babies very close together; about every year and a half she would have another baby. The bitter cold of Montana's winters and the hunger was more than she could bear. Her baby, Paul, was only a few months old when he got sick with pneumonia and died. Mama asked Dad to take her back to be with her own people in Dakota.

They buried Paul out there on the prairie. Then, when the weather got warmer they went back to live near our Indian (DesJarlais) grandparents. We called them Mooshum and Kookum. In Ojibway language that means grandfather and grandmother.

My
North Dakota Home
& Memories

I was three years old when we lived in North Dakota on my DesJarlais grandparent's allotted land, which was located in the Western part of Montana near the border, where the Missouri river joined the Yellowstone River. Grandfather DesJarlais had 160 acres.

More children came. There were nine of us and Mama took in her brother's daughter, Violet, and raised her along with our youngest sister, Gen. They were the same age.

Our house as I remember it, was a three room tar paper shack. We had a lean-to, used as a mud room, and a place to store our water barrels and the wood for the cook stove and the heater. The floors were bare wood pine. We had a large square table in the kitchen, with benches all around, and a cupboard with dishes that came from God-knows-where. We never had a cup with a handle or plates that matched. Everything was used and abused. But, we survived. As I look back, I don't know how Mama kept going. To this day, I have a fetish about dishes and good cookware. I find myself buying things I really don't need but think I have to have.

In our living room/bedroom combination, we had a day bed. It looked like a couch, but it made up into a full sized bed. There was also another bed, a table, a night stand, a dresser, and the big wood heater. Mama never wasted a thing. All old clothes were cut into strips, then braided or crocheted into rugs. These were placed by the beds and wherever they were needed the most. There were five of us children at this time, more came later. The front room served as a bedroom for the kids. Mama and Dad had a room to themselves.

My father's team of horses and cart.

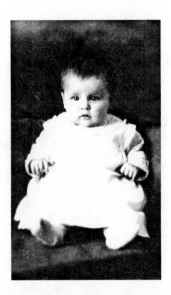

My first baby picture

My brother and sisters
Back row from left to right: Fred, Ursula
Front row from left to right: Mary, Louise, Louella

We are at Grandma Desjarlais in Trenton, ND
From left to right: Mary, Louise, Louella

My Dad's brother, Uncle Phil, lived near us. Dad and Mama took care of him as he had lost his right arm near his shoulder in the first World War. In spite of his pain, he was a lot of fun. He would make fudge for us; it never did harden, but we spooned it or we drank it. It was sweet. He also made popcorn. That turned out a bit better.

Special Times

Those years were hard, but we had our special times. I remember one Christmas Eve during those early years. We were all told to be good. Mama had to get the clothes off the clothes line. It was dark and we had been warned that Santa might be snooping around and we had better get the dishes done. My sister, Louise, who was one and a half years older than I, was bickering about the work. All of a sudden we heard a tapping on the window. Looking up we saw Santa. He shook his head "No, No." We were so scared we ran and hid in bed.

Mama came in with her arms loaded with all these frozen long johns. She had to be very careful weaving in between and around the furniture. One bump would break a frozen arm or leg off the long johns. She finally got them all hung behind the heater. Very soon the steam from these frozen long johns filled the house with the smell of the outdoors, so crisp and fresh.

My sister and I had to stand on apple boxes to reach the table. As we had no indoor plumbing, all water had to be heated in the dish pan and the tea kettle. We had a reservoir on our wood stove, so if we had water in the reservoir, then we had hot water to rinse the dishes.

Mama called to us to get out of bed and get our job done. No way. We stayed under covers until morning. I'm sure, as I look back, my oldest sister who was eleven or so, had to finish our jobs. All of our stockings had been hung with great care and anticipation. We hung them on the bed post, from a drawer or wherever we could find a vacant spot. Santa would figure out whose was whose.

We never had a Christmas tree, but we all enjoyed the one at the school. It was decorated with homemade chains or colored paper and long chains made out of popcorn. We didn't have lights (electric), but we had lots of little candles. We clipped the holders onto the tree branches, and very carefully, the candles were put in. It took a lot of hands to light all these candles. They were lit only

when it was time for the arrival of old St. Nick. Every
child got a little gift, plus the usual candy and fresh
fruit. Every year the pageant of the birth of our Lord
was redone. It was an honor to have a coveted part,
no matter how small.

Our Christmas at home was as exciting as any kid
wanted to make it. We awoke real early, anxious to
see what Santa had given us. In our socks were a pair
of long, black stockings and black sateen bloomers.
In the toe of the socks was an orange, some hard
candy shaped like ribbons, and some mixed nuts.

It was our Uncle Phil who really was Santa. He
gave Mama the money to get these needed items.
He received a pension from the government for his
injuries.

Sleigh Bells to Kookum's and Mooshum's

After a hearty breakfast of oatmeal, we all got
dressed wearing all the warm clothes we could. We
were headed for our grandparents, on Mamas side
of the family, our French-Indian grandparents, we
called them Mooshum (grandfather) and Kookum
(grandmother). Dad hitched up our team to a big
sled. At the bottom of the sleigh box there was a
place to put hay and we had a real buffalo robe to
snuggle under. We were all in a very festive mood
and Dad put all the bells on the harness. It was a trip
to remember.

Christmas Bullets

Soon we were at Mooshum and Kookums. We
could hear the bells from the other sleighs and

people laughing and singing. It was Mama's brothers arriving with their families. The voices and bells rang out in the crisp cold air. After greeting every one, Kookum set the table. The women helped Kookum dish out the food. Mashed potatoes, bullets, gravy, beet pickles, carrots, and for dessert, raisin pie.

Bullets were made of ground-up venison with a little pork sausage mixed in. This mixture was put in a large bowl, with chopped onions, salt and pepper, and flour added. Then, it was rolled into golf ball sized balls which were popped into boiling water and cooked for about ten minutes. When they were all done, a thickening of flour and water was added to the boiling water. This made a gravy, or bouillon. All the families served this meal for special events.

We kids went outdoors to slide down the hill or to just play in the snow. Later, Mooshum would get his violin out and point the bow at one of us kids to accompany him on the organ. He taught us all the chords. We felt so honored if we were picked. Mooshum could not read or write and he spoke very little English, but we kids knew what he meant when he called us "le Job." This meant "little devil" in French.

All too soon, it was time to head for home. The moon was out in all its glory, so bright and big, it was just like day. The snow glistened like diamonds as ice crystals were forming. Far off in the distance, we could hear the coyotes barking. In another direction, other coyotes answered. They had such a mournful howl, downright scary, but we felt no fear. To top off this day, we saw the Northern Lights. If you have never seen this spectacular display, my words cannot describe it.

The Move to Deering

We moved from Trenton to Deering, North Dakota. Dad opened up a butcher shop. He and his brother, Chris, went into partnership. I can still see the meat cases in my mind. My oldest sister, Ursula, had the job of scrubbing out the cases and helping Dad put the fresh meat in. Everything was packed in ice. Peanut butter, pickles and raisins came in wooden barrels. Once, I got into the peanut butter and ate it by the spoonful. I was a pretty sick kid. It took me many a year to get back to eating it again.

My oldest brother, Freddy, was sickly and so was my younger sister, Louella. Mama said it was their hearts. We later learned it was a heart condition caused from rheumatic fever. Freddy went to Medicine Lake, Montana to live with Uncle Joe and Aunt Sarah who were well off. Nice home, indoor plumbing, things we never saw. He needed a place that was comfy, and the food was much better than what we had. We all missed him.

So Ursula, Louise, myself and Louella were left to help out. Louella couldn't do anything. She was so weak. We all loved her so much. We all tried to make her life bearable.

The house we lived in was on the outskirts of town. The house was a much better one then we were use to. There was a big barn and a slaughter house where all the butchering was done.

My Dad was a man that helped anyone that needed help. He took in a colored man who worked for his board and room, helped with the butchering and all the cleaning up. This was the first time we

kids had ever seen a colored man. He was so black,
but his hands were so white. We liked him and the
stories he would tell and his kindness. He was so
helpful to Mama, who was pregnant. She was
expecting her sixth child. My brother, Tony, was born
in November. We stayed in Deering until the next
spring. Then we moved back to Mooshums and
Kookums in Trenton.

Back to Mooshums by Train

We three younger kids, myself, Louise and
Louella, were put on a train at Minot, North Dakota
to go stay with our grandparents until our folks
arrived. Mooshum and Kookum met the train at
Trenton. Their mode of travel was "Old Casey"
hitched to a buggy with fringe on top, no less. Old
Casey was Mooshum's hunting and riding horse, plus
his only transportation. Casey was reddish in color—
a beautiful animal, Mooshums pride and joy. Needless
to say, we kids were not allowed to ride him. The
buggy was a two seater. It had a compartment in the
back for luggage, groceries, whatever. This trip, the
buggy hauled three scared kids and our few
belongings.

We arrived at their home and discovered that
our old tar paper shack was still there, about a half
mile from Mooshums. Our grandparents' house had
been a schoolhouse at one time. One large room, a
kitchen and a mud porch had been added. The one
large room was living, bedroom and entertainment
center. There were two double beds and a dresser
in between at the far end of the building, and a fold-
up bed for company.

Mooshum and Kookum

Red Willow Kinnikinick

At the ends of the double beds, were my grandparents' rocking chairs. Kookum was such a tiny person. Mooshum had placed a box for her to rest her feet on as her feet did not touch the floor. Mooshum had a glider rocker. After the evening meal, they would both light up their pipes "le pip," as Kookum called them. The aroma was so fragrant. I just loved to sit by Mooshum and smell his buckskin clothes, plus the tobacco.

Mooshum would get the red willow for his tobacco from the river bed. He would scrape off the bark, dry it, then he would pulverize it and mix it with store bought "velvet." It smelled so good. Mooshum's tobacco was called kinnikinick.

I must tell you more about the large living room. There was a large heater, and a small table and chairs, another couch-like bed, and the famous old pump organ, so very ornate, with stands on the side to put 2 coal oil lamps so we could see to play. Furniture would be piled one on top of the other when the holidays came. Everybody came to dance, eat and drink. If you could walk, you learned to dance.

Kookum's and Mooshum's bed was the big brass bed with a huge big fluffy mattress made out of duck down. Their comforter and pillows were also made and stuffed with duck down. We dared not look at, lean on, or sit on this bed.

Kookum made her own quilts out of old dresses. Kookum also made all her own dresses. Percale was ten cents a yard at the mercantile store. She traded eggs for her fabric. She also bought flannel and made Mooshum's night shirts and his night cap.

Her house was always so clean. After every meal she would scrub the kitchen floor on her hands and knees. The old pine boards were white after all that scrubbing. Homemade lye soap was all they had to use.

Anyway, when we arrived at their house, we were so scared. We must have had something to eat, but I don't remember. Kookum said it was bedtime. She conversed with us in French and then we went to bed. Soon little Louella started to cry. Kookum told us all to be quiet but Louella was sobbing. All of a sudden we heard a new noise—the big old wall clock with its rhythmic tic tock, tic tock was getting louder and louder.

But another noise was drowning out the clock. What was it? It seemed to be coming from the attic and getting louder. They had an attic in their house with a pull down ladder. It was used as storage for dry products such as navy beans, peas, and all the "love e on shesh" we made. More on that later. We were all real quiet. We kept thinking, if only Mama and Dad were here. All of a sudden, we heard a snorting grunt-like sound. It came to an abrupt halt when Mooshum rolled over, and, his snoring came to an end. Finally, we all went to sleep. We stayed with them for a couple of weeks. When Mama and Dad returned, we moved back into our old tar paper shack. Life on the prairie was again upon us.

Life on the Prairie
From left to right: Tony, Louella, Mary,
Louise, Freddy, Ursula

School Starts

Freddy came home in the fall and we all started school. We had a one room school—students from first grade through eighth in this one big room. We younger kids learned from listening to the older students recite their lessons. Each grade took their turn.

We walked the six miles to school when the weather was nice. We could take a short cut down by the lake. When the weather turned cold, we rode in a cutter Mooshum had made, a sled that we hitched our horse to.

When the weather turned cold, the temperature sometimes dropped to forty below. Then we used the sleigh, as the snow could get quite deep. Our route was longer because we had to go by way of the road, to avoid a railroad crossing.

School was equipped with a barn as some of our teachers also rode to school. We brought grain and hay to feed our animals.

Our teacher was Miss Irwin. She lived on a farm with her parents. She was a large, big bosomed lady. At noon, if you were good, you could have the honor of feeding and watering her horse. Then, when the day was over, we saddled and brought the horse to the front door ready for her to mount.

Well, one day, brother Fred had that honor. As sickly as he was, he had a keen sense of humor, and could play tricks. When four o'clock came, Fred cinched the saddle very loosely. He proudly brought the horse to the front entry, handed Miss Irwin the reins and stepped back. As soon as Miss Irwin put her foot in the stirrup and reached for the saddle horn, over slid the saddle. Miss Irwin was caught off balance. She fell to the ground, and the horse took off for home.

Her audience, the whole school, looked on in wonder and then we all took off for our homes. It was quite exciting. We all wondered what our punishment would be.

The next morning, everyone was quiet in anticipation. Teacher greeted us all in the same manner as usual and after the flag salute, we all settled down to our assignments. I do remember that Dad came to the school to talk to teacher. It seemed funny at the time, but now I don't feel so great about it. Fred was never punished as everyone knew of his illness. He only wanted to fit in and act like a normal kid.

Our Heritage Comes Alive

While living next to our grandparents we learned about the Native Americans, and all the things Mooshum thought we should know. He taught us how to make snares, to catch rabbits, how to make sling shots, how to make whistles out of a willow branch, how to harness old Casey and our own horse to the buggy and to the sleigh, and how to hitch up a team of horses. First, you have to put the harness on—a big feat when one can't reach the top of the horse. We stood on the corral railing. Always, the care of the animals came first.

At this time, we were exposed to other Indian tribes. They would travel from great distances. They were from Minnesota, North and South Dakota, Wyoming and Wisconsin. They would travel one whole tribe at a time. The purpose of their travel was to forage for food. Mooshum's place was a stopping point for any and all tribes sanctioned by the Bureau of Indian Affairs. They always came with a piece of paper from the Indian agency for their area giving them permission to go off their reservation. It all looked so legal, but I don't know if they knew that Mooshum couldn't read. Sign language was the universal language of all the natives.

I use the term "Indian" very reluctantly because back then it was not nice to be Indian. To me, it's a swear word. The tribes all had names, such as Nookota, Lakoota, Sisseton, Bruile, Yanktons and Waphatons. All these tribes belonged to the great Sioux nation.

One tribe in particular, the Chippewas, came from western Wisconsin. There were so many wagons filled with people, young and old. They had many horses, dogs and kids. Mooshum roped off an area to be used as a corral. Some of the horses were hobbled to keep them close by. Deer and rabbits, prairie chickens, grouse and wild ducks were plentiful in the area. We lived next to a lake and grazing grass was lush. On the prairie, it was different, no rain or vegetation.

Our travelers set up camp. They had no buffalo hide tee-pees. History tells how the white man slaughtered the buffalo, not for meat, but for the hide and the thrill of the kill. These tee-pees were made out of discarded army tents. The native women had sewn them with thread gotten at the nearest trading post. We watched in fascination as they set up camp. Everybody worked, except infants. They were put in a cradle board and hung from the wagon in a safe place.

Our new neighbors set up camp in no time, and the women and younger children set out to pick ripe berries. Our land had June berries, choke cherries, wild grapes, ground cherries, buffalo berries and currants. The choke cherry, a small blue-black berry with a pit half as big as the berry itself, was used in making pemmican. This was made from lean, dried deer meat, pounded fine, and mixed with crushed cherries.

The men of the camp went out to hunt deer while the women and children picked berries. The grandparents stayed in camp and took care of the little ones. Deer was killed, cut up in real thin slices and hung out to dry. In a couple of days, the meat would be ready to pulverize for the pemmican. The women would grind up the berries, pits and all, mix the pulverized meat along with a little suet and the berries. These were made into little patties, which were put out in the sun to dry. When they were dried completely and ready to eat, they were stored in cloth bags, where they could get air. This went on every day as long as they were there. On a hunt, one pattie would sustain a person for the whole day. The pemmican was full of vitamin C and protein.

The activities at the camp were fascinating to all of us children. The Native American children, however, were not allowed to play with us—we were not good enough as we were not full bloods. But, we would watch them. Our favorite entertainment was watching them on their horses. What we thought was play were really lessons in horsemanship. How adept they were.

A Gift From Mooshum

Mooshum had a blacksmith shop made out of discarded railroad ties. The building was very low and the roof was made out of ties and had a six inch covering of dirt on top. The soil was real heavy gumbo. When it was wet, it would stick like glue and when it dried it was like cement. Weeds grew on top. The shop was always cool, even in the hottest weather.

We kids would take turns pumping the grinding stone which was a round wheel used for sharpening tools. We would also pump the bellows that were used to heat metals. We pumped both by foot—sitting on a seat like a bicycle seat for the grinder, and standing to pump the bellows.

Looking back now, I'm amazed at how smart old Mooshum was, at mending all the harnesses, wagons and the whole bit. He took pride in his work.

The current visiting tribe was heading for the Rocky Boy Reserve at the foothills of the Bear Paw Mountains. They had a long way to go and needed a lot of fixing on their harnesses and wagons. So, my grandfather was kept real busy.

Soon, it was time for the tribe to pack up camp and head west. They would stop again on their way back. The elder of the tribe gave Mooshum a red pony. She was absolutely beautiful. Mooshum gave the pony to my brother and I. Truly the gods smiled on us that day, as Mooshum usually never gave us anything but hell.

From that day forward, I lived on that horse. Of course, we were supposed to share, but I was older than my brother. We had many a fight over whose turn it was to ride. We named her Goldy. She could out run all those old work horses. We had a lot of races, and she always won! We rode her Indian-style, never had a bridle on, or a saddle, or a halter. Body movements determined her direction.

Annimoose and Honeycomb Ice

Mooshum was given another gift by a different tribe, a hunting dog. His Indian name was Annimoose, and he only knew Indian commands. Mooshum never came back empty-handed from hunting. One day, he was on a hunt down by the Missouri river, and Annimoose was after a deer.

There was a Chinook wind during the night, and the river was melting. At this stage, the ice was honeycombed and very dangerous. Annimoose chased the deer out onto the river. When they both got in the middle, the ice broke and dog and deer went under and the current took them down river. It was sad. Mooshum lost his best friend. He never did get another dog.

The Dust Bowl and the
Great Depression

"Use it Up, Wear It Out,
Make it Do, or Do Without"

We have all done this and we have been the better for it. During the Depression, it was a way of life. Today, we who lived in those days, have a very hard time adjusting to our throwaway society.

In 1930, I was ten years old. North Dakota suffered a severe drought. In addition, the entire nation was hit by the Great Depression. It started out with no rain, wind blowing constantly, the sand blowing in every nook and cranny. Mama would wet towels and stuff them around the windows and doors. It was a losing battle. We ate sand. It would get in your eyes and your lungs. We were later told that our top soil from North Dakota blew as far away as Texas. Nobody had a garden anymore. Trying to keep alive was uppermost in everyone's minds.

Dad decided it was time to move into town. So we left our old shack and we moved into an old two story house right next to the railroad, across the tracks, and near the depot. Our house was close to school, so we didn't have to worry about the weather.

In town was a mercantile store, post office, dry goods and groceries. In the front was a gas pump. Yes, some people had cars—Model A or a Model T Ford. You had to pump the gas by hand, almost like pumping water. Gas was twelve cents a gallon.

When we went to see Kookum and Mooshum, we usually rode our horses. They in turn would come to see us by buggy. As a treat for us kids, Kookum would buy a box of soda crackers and several tins of sardines. This was a treat. We were always happy to see Kookum, but Mooshum could be an ornery old fart. We loved to play tricks on him.

Mooshum and "Le Job"

Mooshum had a post that he carved notches in. This post was made out of a cottonwood tree. It served him well as a scratching post. As I remember it, the carving was on all sides so when he had an itch, no matter where, he could scratch in places that he couldn't reach. He sometimes used it to tie his horse Old Casey to.

One day after returning home from the post office which was housed in the Mercantile store, we heard him rattling down the gravel road. He usually dressed to go to town. This meant he would put on a white shirt, the only one he owned. We waited to see if he would notice that we had painted his post. It was a white calcimine type paint—very hard to wash off. He went through his usual ritual, took the harness off and led Casey to the corral then went back to the hitching post for his long-awaited back scratching and therapeutic massage.

We watched and soon he was aware of his shirt getting stiffer. He looked around for the "Little Devils" who did this heinous deed. We were long gone. He promised us that the Devil would catch up with us and punish us real good. Mooshum really did a number on us as far as "Le Job" was concerned. We would not go out after dark, because if we did, Mooshum said "Le Job" would be waiting for us.

Mooshum gave us a very graphic description of this Devil—red suit, long tail, a head like a goat, with hooves not feet, fire flashed from his eyes. If you looked him in the eyes, which was not likely, you would go blind. Oh my good God, we were scared and prayed to be spared this awful fate that was in store for us.

Well, we went about our usual daily routines. Soon "Le Job," was all but forgotten. Until one night when Mooshum had been gone all day. We figured we were pretty smart. We knew that he was visiting his old friend and drinking buddy. Old Casey knew this routine also and dutifully brought Mooshum home safe and sound. Mooshum stumbled in the house and just dropped the reins and Casey stood still waiting for someone to put him in the corral and take his harness off. Now mind you, Mooshum did not do this too often. It was just dusk, not dark, so Tony and I took over. We led Casey to the corral and as we were just about to open the gate, "Good God" here was "Le Job," leaning on the fence—wickedness glaring at us. I don't remember if we ever got the horse in, and the gate closed or not. To this very day, I will swear on a stack of Bibles that we did see this awful thing, the "Devil," and I hope I never have to see him again.

Cats and Sugar Cookies

Our nearest neighbors were an elderly couple, Mr.
and Mrs. Dan Mitchell. They accumulated cats. I never
saw so many of them—cats all over—on the table, on
all the furniture, everywhere. And the smell—ugh. I
have never liked cats, and I was allergic to them. But
old Dan, as we came to know him, became a good
buddy of mine. He knew I liked to swim, so he often
recruited me to go fishing with him.

Our house was on the bank of a lake. This lake
was formed when the Missouri River changed its
course many years ago. There was a lot of fish, carp
and catfish. This added to our sparse diet. We would
go to the end of this lake where all the tall reeds and
cattails were. I would stand in the front of the boat,
and when old Dan would spear a carp, I would dive
in and retrieve it. This is how he fed all those cats.
The rest of the fish, he gave away. To fish for catfish,
we strung out a net. My Mama would cook the catfish
we caught, and we all enjoyed them.

Tenton Lake, North Dakota

Old Dan's wife was a scary little thing, Her name was Hattie. She didn't like kids and kept to herself. So naturally, we all conjured up all kinds of stories about her; she was a witch, she killed her cats and ate them. We made her out to be a real villain.

One morning old Dan hollered that it was time to go fishing before the sun got too high. He also said he had a treat for us. He had asked my younger brother to come along. We got in the boat, sat down and waited for our surprise. Old Dan opened up his sack. He was beaming as he said, "I made them myself." They were sugar cookies, and boy did they look good. But . . . they were so full of cat hairs! How were we going to dispose of them? "Well," he said, "try them." I took one and dove off the boat. I got rid of mine. I don't know what my brother Tony did with his. We did tell old Dan that we would take the rest home and share them with the rest of the kids.

Town Kids

Now that we were in town, we got to know the town kids. We soon discovered that they, too, thought they were the cream of the crop and we weren't their equals. We were called names, half-breeds, "Mitchiffs." This was so hurtful. My sis, Louise, would go home crying half the time. I put on a good front, but the scars are still very deep.

One family that we were very close to was Mama's best friend, Theresa. She had twelve children, all very close together in age. She had a hard time keeping them fed and clothed. Mama sewed for her children and for us, making pants out of old army uniforms for the boys, and for the girls, jumpers made out of corduroy issued from the good old Bureau of

Indian Affairs. (I preferred pants because I was raised
as a boy—having to do the work of a male member
of the family.)

Mama wanted a boy when she was expecting me.
She had my name picked out, I was to be called
Michael. Well, Michael became Mary—and I was
called "Mike" for short. Everyone called me Mike until
I got married. When my family got together I was
Mike, Dad never ever called me Mary.

There were ten boys and two girls in Theresa's
family. We would all get together and play cards or
go sliding. We made our own fun as they, too, were
considered [damn this word] 'half-breed,' half
French and half Indian.

My dad would tell us all the time that we were as
good as the kids that acted so superior. The majority
of these 'land grabbers' were Swedes and
Norwegians. I can talk with a good Scandinavian
dialect and swear with the best of them, but that
doesn't make me like them any better.

Winter and the Chopping Block

Our winter was quite severe and the government
sent in commodities to feed all the school children a
good meal at noon. Two women were hired to do
the cooking. Lunch was usually ground beef and
venison and barley. Anything that wasn't nailed down
was added to it. It was hot and nourishing. We were
also issued biscuits, a large cracker that was tougher
than shoe leather and took a lot of chewing. But we
all enjoyed this food and I'm sure it was the only
meal many got. We sometimes had a cold biscuit
spread with bacon grease to add to our lunch.

On weekends, my brother and I would hitch up the team and sled down by the river to cut willows for firewood. The willows made a really hot fire that Mama used for cooking. If there was a cottonwood that had blown down, we would drag that home with us. The cottonwood was used in the heater for the front room. Both these trees only grew near the rivers and in the coulees.

Brother Fred came home as often as he could. He always wanted to help. One day he saw the sled loaded with willows and wanted to feed them through while I chopped them into stove lengths.

We had a chopping block, and if your ax was good and sharp it was a breeze. Freddy was doing a good job and I was in the swing of it. It became so rhythmic, I didn't realize there was no more wood left. Fred put his gloved finger on the block and said "Here, chop this," I did. Blood spurted out and with his bad heart, I was terrified. "Oh, dear God, please don't let him die." Mama heard all the commotion and came running out. We all went in the house. Mama stoked up the old wood stove to get the tea kettle to boil. She needed boiled water to mix her healing herbs. She kept a good supply of herbs on hand.

She removed the glove. His finger was just hanging there. She put Fred's finger in place and wrapped it in a bed of herbs. Then she made a splint and secured it with bandages made out of torn up sheets. None of us slept that night. Especially me, I was, in my mind, an ax murderer.

My parents took Fred into Williston to a doctor. He did not lose his finger. It healed in spite of all my guilt and worry.

Dainty

Life went on, it was winter time. I was asked to break a little Shetland pony to ride and to harness for pulling a sled or cutter, as we called them. The people who owned the little Shetland lived in town. They had two very spoiled children, a boy and a girl who was the oldest. Their father was a railroad lineman. He hired my grandfather, Mooshum, to make a sled and to scale down a bridle and harness to fit this little pony.

This task was going to be quite a feat. The snow was very deep but the roads were well packed and very icy. She was a dainty little pony. So, they named her "Dainty."

The big day at hand, I harness Dainty, backed her into the shaft, and got her all secured. She looked at me over her shoulder, real wild-eyed. I told all the kids who were looking on to pile in the sled. When they were all in, I let Dainty have her head. She didn't move very far. She just grunted and groaned.

Then the sled started moving and Dainty started slipping. She looked so scared. One by one, I had the kids get off. As her load became lighter, she became more confident. Soon, she trotted down the road like she had done this every day of her life. Mission accomplished.

Breaking her to ride was much easier. She was bridle broken, she was close to the ground and she was used to having something on her back. I climbed aboard, but she wasn't too happy. I took her out where the snow was deep and she did the usual bucking. I got dumped many times. Finally, she was too tired to do any more bucking. She looked at me as if to say, "You win." We never had any more problems.

Dainty the Shetland Pony

Diphtheria

To top off all the usual wintertime miseries, one
year I got really sick. My throat was so sore and my
fever was so high, that someone told the folks that
they should get a doctor. Mama tried all her
medicines, nothing helped. The depot agent put in
a call to the depot agent in Williston to get a doctor
out.

The doctor came the next morning by train. He
immediately put us under quarantine. Brother Fred
was sent to Montana. Little Louella was sent to
Kookums. Dad went to stay with, I really don't know
who. It seems I had diphtheria.

No one could come anywhere near us for six long
weeks in the coldest part of the winter. People were
good to us as they knew the severity of this disease
and how contagious it was.

Dad checked up on us every day and he would
bring wood and coal and food. The depot agent felt

sorry for us and he would leave the coal bin open at the bottom about six inches so Dad could get enough coal for the day. It was hard coal and burned slow and hot.

I stayed in the front room where the heater was and, as Mama and Louise and Ursula were the care givers, they shared the bedroom. My bed was a leather davenport that made into a bed so I would be warm.

I don't remember too much about the actual illness other than I felt like I was choking all the time. When the swelling went down in my throat and I joined the living, I had no voice. I could not talk for over a year. When my voice did come back, I sounded like a bull frog, real low and gravelly. From that time on, I knew my career as a singer was over. To this very day, I have scar tissue in my throat.

When the time was up and we could all join the human race, it meant a complete house cleaning. Everything that was in the front room had to be burned. This included the leather davenport and the tables. Most of the good stuff had been moved into another room and that room had been sealed off.

I never saw Mama cry during bad times, but I did see her rosary beads slipping through her fingers every time she had a minute to sit and rest. She carried her beads in her apron pocket.

Mary Ann

All was well again and I was alive. Dad went to Medicine Lake, Montana where all his family lived. When he came back in a couple of days, he had acquired some furniture that his brothers scraped together for us.

The best thing that happened was, he also brought a young woman home, one Mary Ann Sayers, who was deaf and dumb as a result of scarlet fever. My mother had gone to school with all the Sayers kids there in Trenton, North Dakota. The Sayers later moved to Montana.

Mary Ann's arrival was indeed a blessing. She was a happy-go-lucky girl and we talked all the time after she taught me how to 'sign.' More on the Sayers later.

Longhorn Meatballs and Raisin Pie

The Depression was on us in full force. People survived by helping one another. Everyone shared what they had.

We had no gardens, the animals were all skin and bones. Our cattle fared a bit better since we lived by the lake, and we had a pasture. Our cattle, horses, and even those big old razor backed pigs, were left to forage. Our milk cows had to be rounded up and brought home to milk. We kept our Indian pony, Goldy, and Old Buck in a corral, or we sometimes hobbled them and let them forage for themselves.

The Bureau of Indian Affairs had herds of longhorned cattle driven up from Texas to feed the starving Indians. We were allocated so many head depending on the number in your family. When they arrived, the cattle were so thin and there wasn't any good grass or hay, only sand and parched earth. Every family got their quota, and to identify whose was whose, paint was splashed on the animal—a different color for each family. Ours were put in the pasture by the lake.

It was my brother's and my job to get the milk cows in for milking and to also do the milking. We weren't very brave and we were afraid of those long-horned critters. One time we went to herd the milk cows in and as we got close to the cattle, the longhorns attacked our ponies.

There was nothing to do but slither off the horses and head for the nearest cottonwood tree. We climbed up as far as we could get . . . scared? You better believe it!! We sat and waited; they made no attempt to leave. So, there we sat.

Dad, in the meantime, was getting anxious, so he cranked up the old Model T Ford and came chugging down the bumpy dirt road, all the while leaning on the horn. The dog was excited and he added to the hullabaloo by barking his head off. With all this going on, the longhorns took off. We hoped they were on their way back to Texas, but no such luck.

With all the rustling going on, the cattle didn't last long. No matter who butchered, they would share with all the neighbors. We all knew that we were not eating our own beef.

Dad butchered a beef and didn't share all of it, as Mama wanted it preserved. So Dad ground up most of it and Mama made small meatballs about the size of golf balls that she fried, and put in a big crock. When she had the crock full, she poured hot lard over them until they were completely covered. Then she would put on a layer of cheese cloth, and a wooden cover that fit very snug. When we wanted some meat, we just took what was needed, the rest was re-covered. The meat balls were put in the oven to heat and to remove the excess lard which was saved for future use.

Lard, powdered milk, canned milk, flour, sugar (sometimes we got grapefruit) were doled out to people the most in dire need. Mama also put up pork by salting it down in a brine. We would get out a slab, cut it up like bacon, then preboil to remove the salt. Then you could fry it and with the remaining grease, you made milk gravy. Our main dessert was raisin pie.

Pickled Pigs Feet

Brother Tony and I would go visit some neighbors who lived about five miles from us. We rode our horses, old Buck and Goldy, the Indian pony. We enjoyed going to see these neighbors, they had a house full of kids all ages, equal amounts of boys and girls. They were kind and really relaxed. If you came at mealtime, you were always asked to eat with them. But first, you had to help with the dishes. After every meal it seemed, everyone got up and left the table with all the dirty dishes and food on the table. So, when the next meal rolled around, someone had to do the dishes while someone else was preparing the meal. This was so remote from the way we were taught.

The father of this big brood was a lazy man. He ate, slept and bossed all the kids from his bed, which was in the front room, along with a player piano. We loved to play the piano. We could pretend we were on a stage with a big audience and the motions we would fantasize, rolling our fingers so adeptly over the keys, in time with the actual player piano's rhythm. Fantasy world was not heard of then.

These neighbors also had a big garden. They planted it in a valley at the bottom of a coulee. So, if there was any rain, it would run down and water the garden. Good planning, and in keeping with their relaxed approach to work. Still, we all wondered how they survived with so many to feed and clothe.

On one particular visit, after we had our meal we decided to go home. Before we left we asked the misses if we could have a dill pickle. This was a treat. You rolled up your sleeves and reached down to the bottom of this big wooden barrel. The pickles would be cured at the bottom. When you retrieved this prize, you could enjoy it all the way home. They were the best pickles I have ever eaten. Perhaps it was all the "earthy spice" from all the hands that had to dig so deep, who knows?

Tony and I and our pickles and horses took a short cut over the hills rather than the road. As we were riding along, we heard all this squealing. As we came abreast of a hill, we saw all these pigs. They were kicking up their heels and rolling around. They would lose their balance and fall down giggling, if a pig can giggle.

We did not know what was going on. We kicked our ponies in the sides and went hell bent for home. An explanation was in order.

We put our horses in the corral, took the bridles off and hurried into the house to ask our dad. We were out of breath and both trying to talk and explain our experience with the pigs. Dad listened and laughed so hard. He was, as he would have said, "tickled all over." He did have a good sense of humor. Gee whiz Dad, "What was going on?" We wanted an answer.

He asked where the pigs were, what area? We told Dad where we saw them, and he laughed all the harder. What we had seen was drunken pigs. It seems like the mash from this neighbor's whiskey still was dumped in that area and the pigs had gotten out and enjoyed the fruit of the vine, right down to their little pickled pig's feet.

We also learned that our neighbor was a bootlegger.

Possibilities...

My Dad's brother from Medicine Lake had written to Dad to see if the Sayers' family could pasture their horses in our pasture. Of course my Dad said yes. After a few days, here came a Mister Sayers and his son with a huge herd of horses. The gates were opened and the horses were driven into the pasture.

Mr. Sayers and his son were a long time in the saddle, three days. They would stop at a farm for the night, where they were fed and their horses also fed, watered and bedded down. Then they would continue on their way again.

At our house, they came in to rest, and wait while Mama stoked up the cook stove. She boiled potatoes and had sliced pork and milk gravy.

I was about twelve and a half years old and became quite smitten with Mr. Sayer's handsome young son. I sat on his lap and kept combing his hair. I don't know why. He was relieved when Mama announced that the meal was ready.

They spent the night and early the next morning, after breakfast, they boarded the train that stopped right by our house. They loaded their saddles, bridles, halters and other things on the train and went back to their home. I never thought about him again until years later. His name was Joseph.

More Lessons...

Now we had to concentrate on our education. We were not happy with all the name calling we had experienced at school. We were not the minorities. This was our land, but they did not want us here. Dad kept us in school saying it would get better.

Another summer went by. Mama's brother had three children. His wife, Dolly, gave birth to another baby. Our little sister, Louella, was back in the hospital again. We had a cousin, a registered nurse, her name was Mary Lou. She took care of Louella who was so sad, as Aunt Dolly and her baby had just passed away. Mary Lou went in to see Louella.

Louella had beautiful curly auburn hair. Mary Lou asked if she would like her hair combed. She also had one gray eye and one brown eye and a mole as big as a dime on her chin. She would always say the doctor was going to remove her mole as soon as she got well. Louella answered Mary Lou by saying no to having her hair combed, and then she said, "Aunt Dorothy died, didn't she? I hurt so bad I don't want to move. I will go tonight also. Don't cry, I will be in a better place." Mary Lou cradled her in her arms. She knew it would not be long.

We lost our dear little sister, an aunt and her baby all in twenty four hours. Ours was a very sad household. We had a large funeral. All were buried on the same day and in the same place. This was a funeral I will never forget. It was in April and flowers were not a part of the landscape in North Dakota. Neighbors and friends made flowers out of crepe paper. They also made wreaths. To this day I hate all artificial flowers, especially made out of crepe paper.

From Left to Right: Mary, Ursula, Louella

My oldest sister, Ursula, was eighteen, and she had a steady boy friend. She was leaving to get married and start her new life in Williston. She married a young man who wrote poems and plays. He had an uncle by the name of Henry Van Dyke, a famous poet. I don't know if one can find his work in the library. This was our only claim to literary fame.

Mama has had two more girls, CeCelia, and our baby, Genevieve. Our family was complete. However, Mama took in a niece and raised her with my youngest sister, Gen, as they were the same age. Her name was Violet. She was Mama's brother's daughter.

Life went on and we all did what we could to make life bearable and to enjoy everyone.

From Left to Right: CeCelia and Genevieve

Hoe Downs and Schottisches

Every weekend we had a big old Hoe Down. People brought food, sandwiches, cakes, etc. All the people were half-French and half-Indian. Music was "life." They were very talented. Everyone played an instrument, violin, guitar, organ, mandolin. The community hall, where all these activities took place, had a piano. Playing was a way of life. The players were self taught and could hear a song and play it immediately. Everybody danced the old waltzes, fox trots, schottisches, polkas, square dances and some of the French dances that were kind of hard to do, but we had fun.

We kids had swimming, ball games, picnics, horse racing and in the summer, we picked the wild berries. We all helped Mama make "love e on shesh"—this is what we called jerky, as you know it. We also made pemmican, the ground choke cherries mixed with the dried meat that was pulverized, then made into patties, dried and stored in the attic.

Ridin' the Rails

Brother Fred came home as often as he could. We were always so happy to see him. He taught me how to ride a freight train. As I look back now, it was so scary. We could have been killed. I realized that after we witnessed a young man get run over by a train. There were so many people riding the rails, going west to look for work.

One day, a group of these boys were kicked off the train right in front of our house. So they came to the door and asked for food. Dad gave them what he could. They went down the hill by the lake, built a fire and had their food. They came back up and sat and visited with Dad. He told them when the next freight would be coming through heading west.

This one young man was intent on getting a job. He was off a farm, and needed money to help his family. Dad had a funny feeling all the while he was talking to the "lad," as Dad referred to him.

Soon the freight train came chugging up this long incline. It was going real slow, as it usually did. When it came abreast of our house, we all watched these young men running to jump onboard. The "lad" missed the rung of the ladder and was thrown under the wheels. Dad ran up to him as soon as the train cleared. His legs were all mangled. One of us kids ran to get an old sheet that Dad could tear up to make a tourniquet and one of us went off to the depot to tell what happened.

On the side track was a hand car. The depot agent called ahead to have the track cleared. He and Dad took off for Williston. Dad held the lad in his arms and he was able to tell Dad where he was from. He asked Dad to write to his people.

When they arrived in Williston, there was an ambulance waiting. They took him to the hospital. Dad stayed with him until he passed away.

Leadership Development

As we lived close to the railroad depot, we became familiar with the engineer, the brakeman and the fellow in the caboose. They would always wave, and shout a greeting. The depot agent had a son about our age. He was a timid little critter and had to be coaxed into helping us with this one "big deal" that we had in mind. We wanted to make a raft, but we needed some long poles.

We saw some poles alongside the grain elevator. Oh boy, what a raft they would make! They were telephone poles, nice new ones. We recruited more help, after all, it was for all our benefit.

It took quite a lot of muscle. After getting them over the railroad tracks, it was clear sailing. We just rolled them to the bank. The bank went down to the lake, I'm sure, well over one hundred feet or more. One push and the poles were on the way to the water's edge, where we then lashed them together with ropes. It was wonderful to have succeeded in such a worthwhile endeavor. We all enjoyed the raft that summer and for many more to come.

That same summer, I became real sick and ended up in the hospital with pneumonia. This was a terrible blow. All the while I was so sick, here these kids were reaping the fruits of all my planning.

The day finally came when I got to go home. Of course my brother and a cousin who was visiting from Montana suggested we swim out to the raft. Stupid me, I was game. We all headed out toward the raft. I almost made it, but being so weak and just out of the hospital, my strength just went kaput. I reached for the raft and hollered "Help!!" The boys looked at me and laughed, "Who does she think she's kidding?" I went down again.

When I was going down for the third time, I vaguely saw both boys dive in and grab me and drape me on the edge of the raft. They pulled up anchor and they paddled in to shore. I lay on shore spewing water and getting dried off. We made a pact not to tell Mama. She had so many worries and didn't need anymore.

Mary—Always ready to cool off in the lake.

A Turn in the Road

Our summer was almost gone. We made the most of our free time. We had many a rousing game of marbles. I was the only girl that could or would play. Commies were the cheapies, made out of clay. The coveted marble was the Aggie. It was made out of agates. We would trade ten Commies for one Aggie.

I used to baby-sit the same kids that had the Shetland pony. Their dad was a lineman on the railway. I liked to sit with these kids because they had "funny books," the Buck Rogers type with way out stuff, the sort of things one couldn't ever imagine coming true—space age travel in space vehicles. Today, we see it all. They also had a radio.

One night, these people had gone out to dinner in town and were going to a movie and said they would be a little late. My Dad had also gone into town to deliver some baby clothes to my sister, who just had her first baby. She had gotten measles and both she and the baby were quarantined.

Dad took the clothes in to her at the hospital. He had ridden in with a neighbor. They stopped to have a few beers before coming home. This old neighbor was such a slow driver and so very cautious that no one could believe that what happened, really did happen.

It seems that they were coming home driving west. As they approached a hill, a delivery truck sped around a stalled car and hit them head on.

My dad was injured so badly that they didn't think he would live. They didn't set any bones or do any corrective surgery. His friend was also injured, but not quite as badly as Dad. Dad was scalped, had his throat cut (just missing his jugular vein), his ribs were broken and his hip was broken. He was one big mess.

His friend also had his hip broken but he didn't have the lacerations and broken ribs. The truck that hit them was a NeHi bottling truck.

Hours later, the people that I was sitting for returned home. It was very late. The father told me he would take me home as he had some bad news to tell my mother. Well, his news was the terrible accident that involved my father. He took Mama back to the hospital and we didn't see much of Mama for a long time. Dad was so mangled, he really didn't know what had hit him.

Dad was in the hospital for over a year. When it was evident he was going to live, they had to re-break his bones and reset them. His ribs were the worst. After resetting them, he had to do breathing exercises.

He asked for his harmonica and blew into it, but there was no music. Gradually he was able to project a semblance of a tune. As time went by, his lungs became stronger. He was playing everything from The Red River Valley to Buffalo Gals.

Dad's hip was damaged so badly that no amount of surgery would ever correct the damage that was done. His right leg was paralyzed. He used to tell us kids that even though his foot was dead he still felt all the pain. He begged the doctors to cut his leg off. They refused, saying that he would still feel as though the leg and foot were there. He used crutches and his right foot just hung down. He had to sort of swing his foot up with every step. We did not understand all his pain.

Growing

My sister Louise and I were sent to an Indian school in Oregon. I can see Dad's reasoning now, why he wanted us to go. Two less mouths to feed and, besides, we were so unhappy with the public school. Plus, the Bureau of Indian Affairs was putting the pressure on my folks. This was one of their methods—break up the family and you break the Indian spirit. So, here we were—being sent to a land I never heard of.

My brother Fred was still in Montana, Tony was left at home along with my younger sisters, CeCelia and Genevieve. It was up to Tony to do all the chores and be the man of the family. He had more burdens than any kid should have had. Life on the old homestead was anything but happy.

We had some free time before we were scheduled to leave the first week in August. We were both teenagers. My sis Louise was one and a half years older than I and was the artist in the family. Even with all the chores I had to do, come dishes time, Mama would call on me to help with the dishes. This was not fair, but we could not impose on a budding artist. She would go out and draw the sunset or whatever she happened to see. You're damn right I was mad, and tired.

Our time at home was drawing to a close, we didn't know what to expect. I knew I wanted to go to Canada to a barn dance before we left. This one girl I knew was married and wasn't much older than I. Dad frowned on the friendship. Why didn't he or Mama tell us she wasn't as nice a gal as we thought?

Anyway, she had an old Model A Ford and she would take the car full of girls only. It was a good 80 miles from our place to this farm in Canada. Big barn, and the hay loft was empty. We did all our dancing in the loft. Oh, what fun, those "mitchiffs" could really play and dance! We packed a big lunch, plenty

of water and left early when the sun was coming up.
After dancing all night, we would head back home
and get home before dark. We realized this was a
little bit much. After all, we had our own Hoe Downs.
It was fun to get acquainted with different people.
Boys. Let's be honest, Mar . . .

Going Away to School

The time has come. Louise and I have our few belongings packed ready for our new adventure. We were being sent as far away from home as possible, to the state of Oregon, south of Salem. The name of this school was Chemawa.

It was the policy of the Bureau of Indian Affairs to bus students away great distances. This was one of the methods used to break up families and kill their spirit. The year was 1936, mid-August. We were taken to Poplar, Montana, 60 miles from our home. At this time an Indian boarding school was in full operation there at Poplar. Students from other far-off states came there, but we were sent even farther away.

As Dad was crippled and couldn't drive, we took the train to Poplar, Montana to spend the night at the Indian boarding school. We were met at the station by a matron. She took us to the dormitory and showed us where we were to sleep and told us when we were to eat. All day long, students arrived from North and South Dakota, Minnesota, Wisconsin and north eastern Montana.

Early the next morning, after a hearty breakfast we boarded a school bus for the start of a three-day journey. We were supervised and looked after by a matron who was a very stern woman, the first of many more to come. We were all excited and looked around to choose our seat mate. I had been in the dormitory with five other girls and the one I chose was a little girl from Medicine Lake. She and I hit it off from the very beginning.

Her name was Rosalie. She was a couple years older than I. We talked about everything; we had so much in common. Everything was so new as neither of us had ever been away from home.

We watched the landscape rolling by, wheat fields all golden and rippling like waves. As the miles slipped by, soon we could see the mountains looming up in the West, how beautiful. We got closer and closer to them. Everything was so green and the snow on the mountain tops was picture postcard perfect.

We entered the city of Missoula, Montana. What a beautiful city. This was to be our first overnight stop. We were served sandwiches and fruit for lunch on the bus. Our bus finally stopped at a motel on the outskirts of the city. Time to stretch and get the kinks out.

Everyone was hungry. Matron had us all get in line and we were marched to a diner. The food was all prepared and there was enough seating space for all of us. Then we went back to the motel and were assigned our quarters for the night. Rosalie and I wanted to be together, that was arranged. My sis Louise had also found a new friend, and they stayed together all through the trip. As they were older, they were in a higher grade and both were interested in art.

Since it was still daylight and would be for quite some time, Rosalie and I decided to look over the town, or rather the area we were in. So we asked

Matron if we could walk about and do a little sight
seeing. She consented, but informed us that curfew
was 8 o'clock. Little did we know, from that moment
on, we would be under the scrutiny of the ever
watchful eyes of a matron. Every action would be
recorded and evaluated.

We took off to see the sights, making sure we
had street numbers and our bearings. Walking slowly
and admiring all the pretty flowers with the green
grass so well manicured, we never saw such well
organized houses and streets all spanking clean.
Rosalie and I were so in awe. As we walked, we talked
and found we had so much in common; we liked to
have fun, liked to dance, in plain English, we were
game for anything within reason.

Gradually we became aware of a car which
seemed to be following us. In the car were two boys
about our age—they were trying to get our attention.
They succeeded in doing so.

They stopped and asked us if we'd like to go for
a ride. The boys seemed so very nice, as it turned
out, they truly were. After we introduced ourselves,
they asked where we would like to go. I, of course,
expressed a desire to see the mountains up close.
The young man driving the car said it was well over
sixty miles, but he would be happy to drive in that
direction. We told them we had a curfew and had to
be back by 8 o'clock.

We talked about our leaving home and where
we were going. They asked why the Bureau of Indian
Affairs had so much to say about us as individuals.
We tried to explain that we were wards of the
government, we had no say over our lives.

Leaving the city behind, we headed for the
mountains. The beautiful green valley nestled in the
foothills, and the big ball of fire setting on the top of

the mountain was a sunset that I will remember always. The boys were concerned about the time, so we headed back. We asked them to let us out a couple of blocks from the motel. We had not been told, but we both had the feeling "dear matron" would frown on our little adventure.

Bright and early the next morning, we continued on our journey. We drove through the same valley we had seen the night before. In the early morning hours, the sun was just rising and casting its rays on the mountains. It was a picture shown from a different perspective. From this point on, I was all "eyes." I could not absorb enough of the beauty that unfolded with each passing mile.

When we reached Idaho, we began to see fruit on the trees. As we traveled on into Washington State, we saw large orchards. To a person who had been raised in a dry, barren land, this was truly the Garden of Eden.

We followed the mighty Columbia River on the Washington side. What were those big berries so black growing for miles along the highway? Someone told us they grew wild and were Cascade berries. We later learned all about them when we got to school, as we picked them, made jam and while they were in season, the boys in the bakery made pies. I still like them, especially the jelly and syrup.

Chemawa

The first Indian boarding school was an old Army barracks, in Carlyle, Pennsylvania. It was a Quonset hut. Captain M.C. Wilkinson, Third Infantry U.S. Army, was the superintendent of the first government school for Indian students. As a result, these schools were run in a military fashion—the marching, the demerit system, issuing Army blankets, towels and shoes, etc.

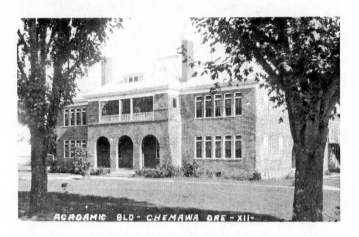

Chemawa Indian Boarding School in Oregon

We crossed over into Oregon and after about a three-hour drive, we reached our destination— Chemawa Indian Boarding School. We were all amazed to see what a big operation this was.

After we disembarked we were assigned another matron. She was the floor matron. All the girls on our bus were assigned to rooms on the second floor. We were shown our quarters by one of the students from the year before. The rooms were large, six girls to a room, and consisted of one cot, a bedside stand and a locker for each of us.

Rosalie and I were roommates. We looked about at the tall windows bare of any curtains. On the bedside stand were two bath towels, a bar of soap, a tooth brush and tooth paste. On the bed was a folded up blanket, two sheets and pillow case. Our guide told us the cots had to be made so we got busy with our bed making. Our guide left us on our own.

Suddenly we heard a shrill whistle, the first of many thousands of times. We six girls rushed to the door and looked out down the hallway. Matron motioned for us to follow her. At the end of the hallway and at the top of the stairs, we all stopped. Matron snapped an order for attention, she looked so stern and fierce. I had the feeling that life on the second floor was not going to be easy.

The orders at that moment were to line up in twos. "When I blow my whistle, we will all march out and go to the auditorium," dear matron stood firm as she looked us all over. I wished I could find a place to get away from the look of contempt that was so visible.

One long blast on her whistle and we tried to march, not really, as no one was in step (that came later). We marched across, past buildings with which we later became familiar. The campus was beautiful, a carpet of green grass all over.

We reached the auditorium and saw other students who had also just arrived from parts unknown. The girls were told to sit on the right and the boys on the left. This would be the procedure from now on. The matron told us her name, we were to call her Miss . . . . I have long forgotten what her last name was. She said she was the second floor matron and all the students on second floor would answer to her. The boys' supervisor gave this same message to the boys.

The superintendent of the school went on stage and read the rules and regulations, our duties, discipline, and our rights, which we soon discovered were non-existent. We were handed brochures of the campus and given a copy of the rules and regulations. We also received a large printed sheet

which explained the discipline procedures. And
that's when I learned abut the Demerit system!

Before we were dismissed, the superintendent
introduced one of the students, a senior who was
studying music, he sang the "Indian Love Song." Man,
it made my "hair stand on end." It was just beautiful.
What a voice. His name was Henry SiJohn.

At this point, we were marched to the dining
hall, which was huge and had a seating capacity of
400. At long last we get to eat. It was nearly 6 o'clock
in the evening. We were assigned our table which
would be ours for as long as we were there. Three
boys and three girls were assigned to a table.

The floor matron left us under the watchful eye of
a much sterner looking matron who was a big bosomed
matriarch. Her "throne" was elevated and she sat up
there with a commanding view of all her subjects.

She reminded me of the story we were told when
we were kids how God had this big book and he
recorded all your bad deeds. Well, she had a big book
and all our names were in it. As she called roll, we
answered, some of the Indian names she could not
pronounce. I always felt I was unduly picked on
because my name was easy to say. The meal was eaten
in silence, we were not allowed to speak other than
to ask for food to be passed. The meal was served
family-style and by students who were living on
campus. Our turn at serving would come later.

We were dismissed via whistle to go back to the
dormitory. The second floor matron would be waiting
for us outside the door. We were marched back. By
golly, we were getting the hang of this marching bit,
and it was only our second try.

Matron gave us a tour of our dorm. We had to
shower, finish making our bed, unpack our clothes

and then we could visit and get acquainted. Lights were out at 9 o'clock p.m. There was to be NO talking after that hour.

It didn't take any of us long to unpack and put our few belongings away. We showered by room number, six girls at a time. If you were modest—which most of the girls were, you didn't shower the first night. No one had a watch or a clock in our room. We knew when we heard that darn whistle that it was time to be in bed.

One of the girls in our room read the agenda for the next day. We had to be up dressed and in line in alphabetical order in front of our dorm at 6 o'clock a.m. Then, we would be issued a worksheet and orders for the day.

We were all very tired and the sun was still shining. There was still a lot of daylight left. After all, it was only mid-August. But it was bedtime. We crawled wearily into our beds.

Suddenly we were struck with the full realization of where we were and the hundreds of miles that separated us from our homes and families. We covered our heads with our sheets, to block the light and to stifle the sobs of homesickness.

All too soon we heard the shrill whistle, time to get up. I scanned my rules and reg sheet and saw that first thing was fix bed, shower, brush teeth, and be fully dressed in thirty minutes. I tossed my reg sheet on the end table and dashed down to get in line. We marched again to the dining hall. Only this time, when your name was called, you approached the almighty at her throne, she handed you your work orders for the day. Then you went back to your table and quietly ate your breakfast. Yes, we could say good morning to our table mates.

We looked our worksheets over. Oh boy, I got to work in the orchard picking fruit. I could eat all the fruit I wanted. I was assigned a former student as my instructor.

The matron called us all to attention. She wanted us to understand that our school was self-sustaining. We grew everything we ate. We canned or preserved everything we ate, so we must all cooperate and work hard. Only when the harvest was over would our academic work begin, and then we would only put in three hours a day.

Louise and Mary at Chemawa

The rest of the day would be spent keeping the plant going. We had a dairy, milk cows and also beef cattle, pigs, chickens, ducks and a few turkeys and horses that were used to plow and haul hay and other sundry chores. There was also a laundry, cannery, bakery, wood shop, auto shop, beauty shop and our very own hospital. The hospital was always filled with Indian people who were ill. If you were inclined to want to take up nurses training, it was there for you. If you were ill and needed care, it was there for you also.

A doctor was within easy reach and a registered nurse was right on the premises. We would all have the privilege of getting our turn at learning any of these trades. The boys did all the dairy work and worked with the animals. We had one vintage tractor. Old Stone Face, as we dubbed our dining room matron, then expounded on the Demerit System. From this day forward, she told us, all our misdeeds would be recorded. We could not socialize with the boys, only on special occasions. We could not go one step west of the bandstand, as that was male territory and out of bounds for the female gender. On the other hand, going east of the bandstand was out of bounds for the male gender. The bandstand was situated right in the middle of the campus. If anyone was caught out of bounds, it resulted in 5 demerits.

The list of don'ts were endless. When you received a certain number of demerits you worked them off to redeem yourself. You did this by doing jobs that were real distasteful and required hard labor—like paste waxing the long hardwood hallways, and then polishing them, cleaning the faculty homes, baby sitting their children.

These demerits were totaled every week, which meant a lot of us were continually redeeming ourselves (Rosie and I kept our hallway polished). If you had a clean slate and no demerits, then you could

go into Salem to a movie. You had to have enough
money, however, to get a ticket. Most of us didn't
have two shekels to rub together. Only the students
who worked for wages had any money. Some of the
tribes were more affluent so their kids had spending
money. Our socializing was nil. Oh well, we had fun
anyway.

Not all the matrons were old buzzards. One we
liked worked in the main office. She would check
the students in and out of the building whenever
they had permission to leave. Rosie and I had no
money, and usually had to be confined to our room.
We didn't even have a radio to listen to. Matron
would come upstairs and get us. We would go to her
quarters and she would make fudge or popcorn. She
was our friend and she was real fair in her dealings
with the students.

Then there was church every Sunday. We went. It
was not our faith, but it did get us away from the
drudgery. And then, too, we could socialize in the
afternoon—boy meets girl—under strict supervision.

There was usually a band concert and a movie in
the evening. The bandstand was situated right in the
middle of the campus. Usually, the band played right
out in the open. This left the bandstand empty so all
the matrons could sit up there and keep an eagle
eye on all the happenings, and usually, something
did. These young people were uninhibited and were
not used to the white man's rule. None of us were
taught the facts of life. You grew up and learned
from nature.

Rosie and I often missed these events as we were
busy working off demerits. It became a challenge to
Rosie and I to have fun without getting caught.

Back to my story. We had arrived on a weekend,

so, come Monday, it was off to work we went. I was
down for picking fruit. Oh boy, I could hardly wait.
First we picked, then we canned the fruit. This went
on until all the fruit was processed. Apples, pears,
prunes and blackberries.

This day we, my guide and I, were in the prune
orchard, picking and eating. As I looked over to the
adjoining orchard, these little fruits, so small and
delicious looking, seemed to beckon "come and get
me." They looked like prunes but were much smaller
and, oh so sweet. I ate my fill and was climbing back
through the fence. My pockets were full and so was
my stomach. My guide spied me and came over wild
eyed and full of fear. "Do you know that you were
out of bounds? Did anyone see you?" Gosh, I didn't
know. This time she said we weren't caught, so don't
let it happen again.

I asked her what these little treasures were. She
said they were called "pettites" and were from the
prune family. She also said that if you ate too many
of them, they were better than any laxative. They
also had the same effect as do beans. She was right.

After all the fruit had been picked and canned,
a truck load of salmon came in and we canned
salmon for two weeks. This was another first for me.
I'd never seen a salmon—and these were monstrous
looking fish.

By now we are getting acquainted with some
members of the opposite sex. The boys worked in
the cannery and did all the heavy work. As they
cleaned and cut up the fish, they were slid down on
a long stainless steel table where the girls packed
the fish in cans and added salt. One or two students
then put the covers on the cans and put them in the
sealer. The boys then put the cans in the pressure

cookers and removed them after the required
processing time. Then the girls would date and label
each can and put the cans in boxes and they were
sent to the storage area. It was hard work, but Rosie
and I enjoyed it.

We liked to work in the bakery. We could eat our
fill of the baked goods. The one job I hated was
working in the laundry. Doing sheets wasn't too bad,
just cumbersome. Especially when it took two people
to run them through the mangle iron (a large
machine with a huge roller that ironed the laundry
items as they were fed into it). It was hot in the
laundry and the sheets were heavy. Ironing shirts that
were starched and wet down to almost dripping was
penance enough. The shirts belonged to the faculty
and the boy students.

This one day, I ironed the same shirt ten times
while the laundry matron stood over me and watched
my every move. When I thought I had the shirt ironed
perfectly, she found a wrinkle and wet the shirt down
again. Finally, the tenth time, by gosh I'd show her. I
was ready to cry, kick, anything to relieve my
frustrations. I'd show her—she was not going to wear
me down. I finally got it ironed to suit her. There
was no praise, she just nodded. I was so tired I didn't
care at that moment.

I can truthfully say I learned TWO things well at
school—to iron a man's shirt and make a bed. I can
miter a sheet corner and make the sheet so tight a
flea would bounce if he landed on the sheet.

As far as academics were concerned, we never
had a chance. The teachers who were hired were
people who could not get a teaching job in the public
schools. These were people they felt were "good
enough" for the Indian students.

Some of the students were very talented, especially in arts and music. These students were bused into Salem for classes. Upon completion of high school, they were given scholarships to an Indian art school in Gallup, New Mexico or a music school in Salem, or Portland, Oregon. Our actual classroom time was about four hours every day. The rest of the day, before and after classes, was spent in keeping the plant in operation.

My sister, Louise, stayed in school and graduated and went on to Gallup, New Mexico to further her art. As for myself, I was plagued with asthma and had regular bouts of same, so it was decided I would go home. I was at Chemawa for over one year. I have since been back to visit twice. The last time was in 1975. Things have changed for the better. Most of the faculty are Native Americans and a large percentage had been students there themselves. They can identify and know first hand the needs and the spiritual needs of the peoples.

Chemawa School Board now consists of all Indian people. This is good and the way it should be. The school board members represent Alaska, Western Washington, Oregon, Idaho and Eastern Washington. These are the major areas from which the Indian students come today.

Back Home Again

I was gone a little over a year. It seemed like a lifetime. So much had happened. I learned a lot and had grown in strength and even academically. It was good to be home, as I worried that everyone's health had deteriorated. Dad was drinking more and more. Mama was also drinking. As I am older now, and

looking back, the life we had would drive anyone to
drink. So darn poor and the depression in full swing.
We could not see the light at the end of the tunnel.
Aunt Alice in Medicine Lake, Montana wrote and
asked if I would come and stay with Uncle Chris, my
dad's brother, to help with the cooking and do
housework, so she could go to work. She was hired
as an instructor to teach the women how to cook the
food that was given to them. She also taught them
how to sew. Uncle Chris had suffered a massive heart
attack and could not do anything. Aunt worked long
hours at her job. If I came, she did not have to worry
about Uncle being alone. This setup was designed
to help us all.

I found the work helping my aunt and uncle very
pleasant, as they were so easy to get along with. Then
there was cousin Bernard, their only son. He went to
high school, and on weekends ran the movie
projector at the local theater and was active in all
school activities. When it came to sports he was a real
"klutz." Their only daughter Phyllis was in College at
Helena, Montana. She chose a teaching career.
Bernard went on to medical college and he became
a Doctor of Pathology. Theirs was a different lifestyle
than I was used too. They never made me feel like a
poor relation though, and Bernard became my good
friend.

A Small World

One day, Aunt Alice came home from work and asked me if I would like to go and visit with their neighbors, the Sayers, who lived about five blocks from them on the top of the hill. Aunt told me that they had lost their daughter Rosalie. Aunt said it was the same Rosalie I knew at the Chemewa boarding school and maybe I could cheer up Mrs. Sayers by telling her about our school days. I was so surprised to hear that Rosalie had passed away. I did not realize Rosalie was sick. I had heard that she had tuberculosis of the throat. She spent a lot of time in the hospital at school. I just thought she was interested in nursing. She must have left school shortly after I did. I later learned that she was sent to Tacoma, Washington to the Cushman Indian Hospital, then sent back to the Poplar Indian hospital where she died in April of 1937.

The Cushman Hospital was a large brick six story building situated on the Puyallup Indian reservation in Washington. It served all of the Indians from the western states. The top floor was used as a tuberculosis sanitarium.

I went up to see Mrs. Sayers. She seemed to know who I was and why I was there. I knocked at the door and a girl about my age opened the door and invited

me in. She said her name was Ann and took me in to
where her mother was sitting. Mrs. Sayers was happy to
see me and asked questions about Rosalie. We did not
communicate too well as she spoke very little English.
This was in early fall. Ann asked me to go to a movie
with her on the weekend, in town about a mile from
their house. I asked Aunt and she thought it was good
idea. My life would never be the same again.

When the appointed hour came, Ann was to stop
by and we were going to walk downtown. Well, here
came this car and it stopped by the gate. Ann got
out of the car came in the house and informed me
that her brother was going to give us a ride to the
theater. He worked in the C.C.C. and usually came
home on the weekends.

> Note: In 1933 President Roosevelt had
> launched the Civilian Conservation Corps
> known as the C.C.C. During the depression,
> this work relief program employed men who
> needed work and money. They were paid a
> sum of $30.00 a month. This money gave
> these men a feeling of self worth. They
> restored public lands, felled trees, built roads
> and earthen dams, worked on projects to stop
> soil erosion, and flood control, built the roads
> and trails and the state parks. Over 2.5 million
> unemployed men served in the C.C.C.

I was not going to go in the car. I told Ann that
was not part of our bargain. No, I was not going to
go. Aunt Alice said, "Go on, you won't have to walk."
She persuaded me to go. I agreed to ride with them
and Ann introduced me to her brother, Joseph. We
got to the theater, and being a gentleman, Joseph

hurried in ahead of us and bought the tickets. He made damn sure he sat right next to me. I will never forget the movie as I had seen it before. It was a war picture titled, "They Gave Him A Gun." I saw Joseph every weekend; we went dancing, or to visit his relatives for some rousing card games of Pinochle.

It was time for me to be moving on. The weather was getting colder and I was needed at home. I went back to North Dakota. Joseph courted me all that winter. It was quite a drive in all that snow and bitter cold. I must say he was persistent.

He got a job in Poplar, Montana with the C.C.C. Indian Department. He was a foreman in mechanics, and kept the trucks in running order, and ordered parts. His pay was only $35 a month. At this time he joined the National Guard which meant a few more dollars. This was important as we were talking about getting married. Joseph lived with an aunt of his there in Poplar.

**Joseph Comes a
Court'n in 1937**

**Mary living in
Medicine Lake, Montana**

Independent Spirit

Spring came and I went to work for some friends who lived in the city. They farmed land that was in Montana where they also had a home. They only lived there during planting and harvesting. They needed someone to help cook and clean and run herd on their little girl as the mother was sickly. I would go home on weekends. I worked for them for two months. I earned $10.00 a month. This would help as I needed some new clothes.

Joseph wrote to me and invited me to come to Poplar and we would go to the Rodeo in Wolf Point. This was an annual event and one of the big events of the year. He was going to come and get me but he had to work a half a day and by the time he came and we got back, the big event would be over. He sent me a train ticket, and said he would bring me home the next day.

I asked my parents. Dad said it was okay, but Mama said I could not go. I was real upset and didn't have much time to try to talk Mama into agreeing. So I said I was going—Mama said, "If you go, don't ever come back." I had spent all my earnings on some much needed clothes. I packed all I had and all too soon the train came.

I boarded the train, and sat listening to the wheels, which seemed to say, "Don't come back"—"Don't come back." This was supposed to be a fun time for me. I cried all the way but I made up my mind I was not going to go back.

The train got to Poplar and I looked around for Joseph. He wasn't there. But there was a real handsome young man who came up to me and asked if I was Mary. I said I was. He said Joseph had to work a little later and had asked him to come and meet me and take me to Joseph's aunt's house.

When we got to his aunt's place she was expecting me and made me feel welcome. I felt somebody cared. So I shed my cloak of sadness, and looked forward to a good time, tomorrow would take care of itself.

Joseph had a lot of relatives and they had made arrangements for me to stay with his Uncle Chick and his wife Mary. They had three or four children and were quite cramped for space. That didn't worry them though, as they were happy-go-lucky people; what was theirs was yours. Mary was from Canada and was more French than Indian. Her maiden name was Dionne. Remember the famous Dionne quintuplets? These were her relatives.

Joseph arrived and got cleaned up. With a car full of his relatives, we set off for Wolf Point. I was to see my first rodeo and honest-to-God Indian pow wow and attend a country dance. This big event always took place on the fourth of July week end. It was fun and all that I had expected it to be. I met so many of Joseph's relatives, time just flew. We were out almost all night. When Joseph finally asked me if I was ready to go home, I told him I wasn't going home.

He didn't ask any questions, he talked to his aunt about a place for me to stay. She found a relative that I could stay with. The next day I went to scout out the town. Joseph was at work, I supposed. I saw this new drive-in restaurant. I went in and asked if they were hiring. The boss himself answered my query.

Yes, they were looking for help. He did not ask if I had any experience and I didn't volunteer. I was to report for work the next day.

The owner's name was Mr. Mitton. He was also the owner of the only dry goods store in town. The store carried everything. His wife was the brains behind the whole operation. I was new in town and young and very confident. But I was green as grass, I didn't even know how to make change. I fumbled through. I will never forget the look on this one Indian's face as I counted out his change. He had given me $10.00 and the hamburger was 35 cents. It sounded good to me the way I was transacting this big purchase—so-o-o-o sophisticated, I counted out his change. My business skills must have left a lot to be desired because Mitton immediately took me aside and gave me a crash course in making change. I know I really got the best of that deal. The drive-in was doing a lot of business. By coincidence, the guys that Joseph worked with and those he knew were all curious to see the small town and new gal in town.

Really, Really Married

Mary & Joseph

When Joseph got off work we had to do some planning. We talked marriage, but knew that we couldn't get married in Poplar as neither one of us was from that Parish. It was unheard of not to get married in the church. So I went to see the local parish priest. He was a gruff little fellow and was used to unwed and pregnant gals coming in to get things done right.

The first thing he asked me was "Do you have to get married?" I told him no. He knew we were not from his parish. The only way he could marry us, he said, was if we first got married by a Justice of the Peace. That would not be legal in the eyes of the church, but heaven forbid, we would be living in sin, so then he would have to marry us properly. And he planted the seed.

The next day we went to the Justice of the Peace, made an appointment, got Chick and his wife Mary to be our witnesses and got married the first time. That was July 23, 1938. Next, I trotted myself back to see the little Padre. He had a few more very important details that needed prompt attention, such as birth and baptismal certificates. I knew I could call the Rectory in Williston and have mine mailed in to Poplar. This I did immediately. After consulting with Joseph's aunt, she was sure we could drive to Culbertson, go to the rectory and get the needed documents for Joseph. So away we went. Back again, documents in hand, we took them to the Padre. One more step though. He had to send them to Great Falls to the Bishop to get a dispensation so we could marry in the Poplar Church, "Our Lady Of Lourdes."

One week to the day later, I stopped in to see Padre. Did it come? "Yes," he said, "If you bring your

witnesses I can marry you this afternoon." We got
Chick and Mary and had the shortest and smallest
wedding ever performed in that church, only four
of us.

Now we were really, really married and legal. The
date was July 30, 1938. No bands, no party, no cake.
We embarked on our life together. It lasted 60 years.
I was eighteen years old.

We wanted to share our happiness with our
family, so we drove to see Joseph's parents and some
of my relatives in Medicine Lake, Montana. The next
weekend, we drove to North Dakota to see my
parents.

We were given a few of my belongings, and had a
nice visit. Mama was quite cool towards me. She was
hurt when I left and I did not realize how she felt.
She felt I was too young. That's what it was all about.
We spent the night and returned to Poplar the next
day.

A Home of Our Own

Time to look for a roof we could call our own. No
more living with relatives. We bought our own home,
a little house right next to the highway. It was small,
but would do for then—one bedroom, kitchen, living
room and wonders of wonders, we had electricity
and running water. We had no indoor plumbing, but
we had a very well built outhouse, built by the C.C.C.
No tricksters would ever push it over, come
Halloween. We made payments of $12.00 a month,
for a total cost of $650.00. Now days that won't even
pay one months rent.

Soon, we were expecting our first child; we had
three children in three years. I learned in a hurry

where babies come from. Our first little girl was born April 21, 1939. We named her Shirley Rose. Rose in memory of Rosalie, Joseph's sister, my friend and roommate in boarding school.

One year later, on April 9, 1940, we had our little Patricia. Another year later we had our first boy child on March 27, 1941, William John Sayers.

Our little house was bursting at the seams. Imagine having two babies on bottles, one toddler and all the diapers and no washing machine! I don't remember ever crying or feeling sorry for myself. I didn't have time for that. I loved my babies so much. The thing I hated the most was having to get up in the night, build a fire in the woodstove and heat the babies' bottles, then get up and cook breakfast. I prayed for Dear God to give me strength—and He did.

Our first home in Poplar, Montana (1939)

Mary and Shirley

Mama Goes Popeyed
Over Flannel Popeyes

Joseph's Mother had a treadle sewing machine, a Singer, which she loaned to me. What I knew about sewing was pathetic. Well, flannel was only 12 cents a yard. I bought 10 yards, no pattern and I sewed up a storm. The print had big characters of Popeye. I made pajamas and nightgowns for my babies. We went to North Dakota to visit my parents. I was so proud of my sewing abilities, and to be able to show my Mama my handiwork. Mama was such a good seamstress. When bedtime came I dressed my little darlings in their new night wear, and showed them off to their Grandma. Well, my mother laughed and laughed. My feelings and my ego were shot down the toilet.

As I look back on this traumatic episode, it must have been funny, these little babies all looking like Popeye. Mama later explained to me you always use small print or small characters on fabric for an infant. I was self taught in anything I ever tried to do.

The War Years—
1941 and Onward

Joseph came home from a National Guard meeting. The Officer in charge had made an announcement that we were at war and anyone with little ones should get out of the Guards immediately. Those who did get out would be needed in defense work.

Training for those young men enrolled in defense work was available at the agency, especially in welding. Joseph signed up for the welding course. This was a six week course. As soon as it was completed, he and three other men headed for Portland, Oregon where the call was out for war workers. One of the men had relatives in Seattle. They stopped to visit, but got no farther as defense needs were so great at Puget Sound Navy Yard in Bremerton, Washington. The men applied and went right to work.

The next step was to find housing so the families could come and make a home as these men were working two weeks straight without a break.

The men arrived in Bremerton the second week

in April. They commuted from Seattle for two weeks
before they finally found some cabins that had been
hastily put up. The cabins rented for an exorbitant
price. The cabins were about 14 feet x 14 feet. They
were furnished with a woodstove, bunkbeds, table
and two chairs and came with a view of a lake. There
were no washing facilities, and on one end of the
building was a shower and toilet. The cabins were to
be used by six families.

When the families arrived, we were given a few
pieces of toilet paper for each family and green wet
wood for the cookstove. It was the type of stove that
you would see in campsites—real small and impossible
to cook and keep warm! The cabin was likened to a
sweat box.

The men had the above accommodations ready
for us. We women, the wives of these four men, drove
out together with our babies. I did not bring my two
little girls as everyone said this war would be over in a
couple months. Wrong. Anyway, I left my little girls
with Joe's parents. Shirley was a little over two years
old, Patty was a little over one and John was about
three months old. I did not see my little girls for
almost a year.

We settled into our little cabin. We four women
had a car between us so we could take off and go
shopping. We all came from flat wide open country
and this forest was more than we bargained for. At
that time, the roads were not much more than an
old cow path. We went looking for the big city of
Port Orchard. No sun, so we couldn't depend on
"ole sol" for guidance. We finally got to the store. It
was built right over the water.

We learned that it takes more than money to buy
food. We had to sign up for tokens, little red ones

for meat and dairy products. We were issued tokens and some script. I needed Karo syrup and canned milk for my baby. Everything was rationed and the town people were given preference over us migrant workers. Even if I had tokens, I was not on their list. Butter was a commodity that one would die for, so my life was spared. I got white margarine instead, in a bag with the little yellow pill that you had to break and stir in for coloration. That white stuff was a far cry from butter but it worked, and didn't taste too bad.

Bremerton Navy Ship Yard

Life in
Port Orchard, Washington

We women decided that we had to have more suitable housing. So we took off to look for anything that had a roof, and was closer to town. People were pouring in, ready to do their bit to help win this war. They too were looking for housing. If you found a house or apartment, the rent was sky high. People rented out chicken coops and asked for and got the price they wanted. I found a house in the Retsil area. It was a one bedroom, sparsely furnished in a run down neighborhood. The one good point it had was that we were real close to a ferry. It was just a matter of walking down the hill to catch the Annapolis ferry. The Veteran's Home was the main attraction, a very impressive building with a beautiful view of the mountains and right across the inlet from the Navy Yard. The veterans had everything they needed to make life pleasant for them.

Our landlady was capitalizing on this get-rich-quick scheme. Everyone was overcharging, there was no rent control at this time. The neighbors came to see me about a very serious problem, it seems our septic tank was over flowing right in their yard. It was really a big stink. I went to see the landlady, who said it was our problem. I didn't know what to do. I walked down the hill to go to the grocery store. I was sure the store owners could advise me. I was pregnant again and having to carry my little boy and all the groceries up and down the hill was a chore. John was too small to walk very far, so I ended up carrying him most of the time. The store owners said they would call the Health Department and inform them of the problem. It wasn't too long before they came out to investigate. My landlady was really upset with me. The neighbors had turned her in numerous times without any results. This time she had to get it fixed.

My younger sister, CeCelia, came out in the early fall from North Dakota. She went to work in the Navy Yard as a messenger girl riding a scooter delivering messages to the different shops. She was a pretty girl and turned many a worker's and sailor's head. She had to quit her job and accompany me and little John back to Montana. War was in full swing. There was only one hospital in town and all the younger doctors were being sent overseas. The older doctors were so swamped and they would not come to the home for a home delivery. Being pregnant, I really had no choice. Sis and I left Washington by train in the middle of February. My due date was the first of March. I had no other choice than to go back to Montana and have my baby in the government hospital.

I Get to See
My Little Girls

The train trip was quite an experience. Troops were being sent to various places for training. The train was packed with young men in uniform. One look at me in my pregnant condition, the biggest and longest look at my sister, and the boys took over. They made a bed in the luggage rack above their seats and placed my little John up there. They asked for and got milk for him. They made room for me and Sis and after we were all situated they stayed up all night playing cards and keeping an eye on us. They succeeded in getting my Sis involved in the card games, and getting acquainted.

The train stopped in Spokane for a half an hour, time enough for these boys to hop off and get sandwiches. There were Red Cross workers lined up along side of the train with food, as this train had no dining car. It was strictly a troop train. How we ever got on, I do not know. At the time I was too miserable to even care. At one point I thought I'd have to get off the train as I was having labor pains, but knowing how long it took me to birth my babies, I felt I had lots of time. We arrived in Poplar in twelve more hours. I did not want to waste any more time, I wanted to see my little girls.

The big arrival—finally we get to Poplar after midnight. What a welcome! A raging blizzard, snow drifts two, three feet high, and even higher were piled up all over. There was no taxi. The dray man, a jack of all trades, was the taxi, delivery man and whatever else he was called on to do. But he did not meet any trains or haul anything after the sun went down.

We could not leave anything at the depot as we were not sure it would be there in the morning. So we picked up our luggage. I got my massive bulk upright, and with John on one hip and suitcases in hand we tackled the drifts, ice and wind. The little one inside was kicking up a fuss. Didn't he know I was having one hell of a time just trying to stay upright and on my feet? It was over one mile from the depot to our little house. The closer we got the lighter my load seem to be. Soon I would be able to touch, hug and have my babies all to myself.

Finally we reached the house. Sis and I stashed the luggage on the back porch and quietly opened the door and went in. I turned on all the lights. I saw this large fold-up bed and two little girls waking up with such a surprised look. We put John on the foot of their bed and I reached over to wrap them in my arms, my tears of joy dripping on their little faces. Needless to say this was beyond their comprehension. "Don't you know me." I asked, "I'm your Mother?" They looked at me with those big black eyes and said in French. "No, our mama and daddy is at the west coast." They proceeded to call me aunt but in French. My babies did not speak English. I dared not cry. So I was another aunt for some time.

With all the excitement going on, we woke up Joe's parents. They came out of the bedroom and greeted us warmly and offered food. We did not refuse. Little John was hungry, none of us had eaten any solid food for two days. Sis went in the bedroom to crash while I was content just to feast my eyes on my two little sweethearts. They thought John was cute but did not associate him as a part of the whole. I became a whole person at last. I made a promise never, ever, would I leave my babies again, come hell or high water.

I spent the rest of the night trying to make my daughters understand me. I crawled in their bed, soon they were in bed with me, jabbering like a couple little magpies. Even if I couldn't understand them, I felt their warm little bodies next to mine, MY LIFE WAS COMPLETE.

The next morning everybody was tired, no sleep, and the excitement of being with my babies was almost all I could bear. My Sis stayed with us another day, then she took the train to go back to North Dakota. She and I have been really close all these years. We share many happy times and memories. When you come from a large family you bond with the one nearest your age. You find that with the younger siblings and the older siblings you have nothing in common with them other than blood ties. CeeCee went home to North Dakota, leaving me to become reacquainted with my little family.

We were all crowded in our little house, the home we bought before the war broke out. When we left to win the war, we left Joe's parents in charge of our home and two daughters. Well now I was back and after I had my new little member, I wanted to take all our family back to Washington State and continue our lives.

Poplar, Montana
Shirley and Patricia

Time was now my bug a boo. I wanted the weather
to calm down. It was now the first of March and my
time was getting closer. The baby was due any time,
the sooner the better, I thought, so we could all go
back to our home in Washington. I hadn't heard from
Joseph for weeks. He was also worried as he hadn't
heard from me. It seems the day after we left
Washington, they had one of the worst snow storms
ever recorded. Everything came to a complete stop.
No mail, no cars on the road, the Navy Yard was shut

down. Joseph walked into Port Orchard and stayed with a fellow from Poplar. However, the Navy Yard was closed down so nobody went to work. I had been gone two weeks before I heard from him. When I found out the reason he didn't write, all was forgiven.

I was making headway with my girls, they were to call me Mama and to speak in English. One morning after we had breakfast, the girls were standing on boxes helping me do dishes. I had been having cramps? Labor pains ??? The weather was up to its old tricks, winds and snow, and biting cold. Joe's dad came in the kitchen and realized I was in labor. He insisted he call the dray man (our local taxi) to take me to the hospital. The snow drifts were so big and the road so icy, no way could I make it on my own. We were only six blocks from the hospital. I told him I could wait a little longer as I knew it would be awhile yet. About that time I doubled up with a huge pain. I hung on to the sink until it passed. My two little girls looked up at me and asked, "What's the matter mama, you got belly ache?" With tears running down my cheeks I told my father-in-law, "Now you can take me to the hospital."

My babies called me mama—the first English they had ever spoken. My father-in-law walked downtown to get the dray man. I went to the hospital in style, though it's a wonder the pickup didn't shake this baby out. No such luck. Three days of intensive labor followed with no doctor, only a midwife. She was a jewel but it did not make it any easier. Finally our son, Tom, was born. It was nip and tuck. He came into this world almost dead. He was a dark blue and the cord was wrapped around his neck. As they were unwinding the cord, I counted one, two, up to nine. The midwife had a nurse's aide helping her. She went and got two large pans, one with cold water and one with warm water. My baby was dipped in one first than the other. Finally they got a little squeak out of him. At this time, Joe's aunt who was the cook, came in the delivery room and gave me care. The midwife and nurse's aide were working over number two son. He was alive and I was completely spent.

How I envied the young Indian girls who came in, gave birth, and in a couple hours they and baby were on their way home.

Manchester Highway

I heard from Joseph. He was so busy and happy to hear all is well with our wee one. He tells me in his letter that he has purchased a piece of property, five acres right on the Manchester highway. It had a lot of timber, and the beginning of a house. The framework was up and the potential was there. Joseph worked like a beaver, he wanted his family with him as soon as possible. It took me a while to regain my strength, and as soon as I could travel two months later, my in-laws accompanied me and my four babies back to Washington and home.

Joseph built a garage and added two bedrooms onto the house. Not finished, but we had a roof and the rest of the summer and fall to make our home livable. He concentrated on the garage, as that would be living quarters for his parents. He made a real cozy little apartment, with a bedroom and sitting room area with a wood heater to keep them warm and cozy. They had all their meals with us. Grandma was a diabetic, which made cooking a little more difficult.

The government bought half our property to build housing units for the shipyard workers and to

house the servicemen's families. Today it is a complex
of modern homes called South Park.

Grandma (holding family friend) and Grandpa Sayers
From Left to Right: Shirley, John, Tom, Patricia

"Pissy Willies"

Joseph and his Dad harvested the trees for
firewood. Our little ones were busy exploring. There
was so much confusion in our backyard—workers
digging ditches, laying pipes for water and sewer,
two story apartments and all the buildings going up.
It was hard to keep track of my little ones. We did
not fence in the yard as there were too many other
priorities.

Our next door neighbor was a sweet little old
lady who never had any children. She was always so
prim and dressed so dignified. I felt like I was so
beneath her, my early childhood rearing its ugly head.
Will I ever get over this feeling?

There was a green belt separating our houses,
large conifer pines. Mrs. DuBois had planted French

lilacs, and pussywillows that had real large kits. My
two little girls were familiar with the pussywillows as
they grew wild in Montana. So they come in the
house beaming. They said, "Here mama, we got you
some "pissy willies." Every spring when I see the
pussywillows in bloom, I see these two innocent little
girls with their offering, they picked them out of love.

They picked as many pussywillows as they could
reach. What a wonderful gift, I was so pleased. My
joy did not last very long. Here comes my prim and
proper neighbor, with malice in her heart. She tells
me that these pussy willows were very expensive, that
they were not your common old wild ones, these were
cultivated. I apologized and said it would not happen
again. I explained to the girls that was a "No-No." I
never heard any more complaints. The girls had to
ask if they could play in the shade of her trees. She
was very friendly from then on.

Grandpa's Fired

One Sunday, Joe's mother, myself and the two
girls drove to the foot of the hill to a grocery store.
We left Grandpa in charge of the boys, baby Tom,
who was sleeping, and told him to especially watch
John. As he was real inquisitive, with all the building
and trucks and general commotion it wasn't safe for
any child. We had a little black and white dog, who
was real good with the children and was John's
constant companion.

We did not stay very long, got our groceries and
came right home. All the stores were open seven
days a week and people worked on Sundays. While
we unloaded the car, the girls went to find John. He

was nowhere to be found. Panic set in—there were so many dangers out there.

Grandpa was fired on the spot as a sitter. He had been reading the paper and just forgot. He started combing the project, calling John's name and asking all the workers if they had seen a little boy and dog. No one had, but they stopped their work and helped in the search. We all came back to the house and didn't know what else to do. So we prayed.

I looked over to the side of the garage. I thought I'd seen the tall grass move. There was a ditch. I went over to investigate and at the bottom of this ditch was our little John. He and the dog were sleeping. Our prayers were answered. We had no telephone, Joseph was working, I had no idea of how to get hold of him. All's well that ended well!!! No, we really didn't fire Grandpa, we needed all the hands we could get and eyes too.

We did get a phone installed, a four party line. I didn't know too many people but felt more secure having this phone. I had a lot of relatives, on my dad's side, living out here but hadn't contacted them yet. They lived in Bremerton. They too were busy with families and housing. My favorite aunt and her family and their children came to this area and established homes. We did not lack for family. Then too, Joseph's parents were here and soon Joseph's youngest brother Ernest and his wife came and settled in the Bremerton area.

Getting from town to town was not that easy, as gas was rationed and you had to make every trip count. Joseph bought an old Model A 1932 Ford four door. He drove this car all the while he was building our little house. It was easy on gas and made a good

truck and my shopping car. Joseph rode the bus to
work as he worked swing shift.

Torpedoes and Ferries

One of the scariest times for me was my first trip
to Seattle. Joseph finally had a day off. We decided
to go to the big city to take in a movie, have dinner
out, and just be free spirits for the day. This would
be the first time I would ride a ferry and leave my
babies home.

We took the water taxi from Port Orchard to
Bremerton, then boarded the ferry, the Kalakala, a
real streamlined metal ship. Kalakala means "The
Flying Bird" in the Chinook jargon. All the ferries
have Indian inspired names, names taken from the
culture such as birds, fish, animals, etc.. The ferry
was loaded, mostly walk on passengers. The bottom
deck was for cars. The middle deck was for the walk
on passengers, with lots of seating areas, and a snack
bar. If one could get close enough to order, it was
first come first served. I was so excited, the water all
around, everything so green and pretty. The crossing,
we were told, would take an hour. We could see
Seattle, it didn't seem so far. I was okay as long as I
could see land all around. But when the ferry came
to a complete stop, I became panicky. Why were we
stopping? One of the regular patrons told me that
this was the usual procedure, as there were large
steel nets strung across this narrow area. They were
there to stop and trap any torpedoes or enemy
submarines if there were any in the area. Japan
wanted to blow our Navy base to kingdom come. We
were never told if any were intercepted. However,
we did hear how close they came. One torpedo came

onto the beach in Oregon close to our friend's home. However, it did not explode. It was detonated and a monument put up on the spot. This was in the Warrenton area, close to Astoria, Oregon.

Stempie

Life chugged along. The routine was caring for our family, in-laws, and sundry pets, such as rabbits. The rabbits weren't really pets, they were a main part of our diet. The children were not allowed to play with our food. Meat was hard to get and we were used to doing without. We planted a garden, they were called Victory Gardens then.

All of this farming bit was inspired by a neighbor who came to Washington from California, and she urged us on. I knew what farming was all about— WORK. I did not realize one could garden in such a small space. Stempie, as my babies affectionately called her, was a grandmotherly old soul. She had left an abusive husband and vowed she would change her life by leaving the father of her children. She told me stories of the abuse, things I could not understand. We became very good friends. She longed for her grandchildren, who were in California. So we shared our babies with her.

Stempie loved our little Tom. One day, when he was only 10 months old and was crawling, we couldn't find him. Pretty soon, we saw our neighbor coming over with Tom in tow. This little boy had crawled over to her house. We had a well worn path between our houses, with one house in between. The path was on top of the embankment, next to the highway. She said she heard this little noise like someone at the door. She looked out but didn't see anything. She heard this noise again, she opened the door and here was little Tom. He knew where he was going. She scooped him up in her arms and the bond was cemented for life. From then on he was her little pal. Sugar was rationed. Stempie would save sugar for weeks so she could bake Tom a cake. She made all his birthday cakes, even after we moved to the farm.

Her name was Helen Stemple. She had a small lot, raised a big garden and had a cow. We bought milk and eggs from her. She taught me the finer points in crocheting and tried to teach me to tat. I never mastered that skill.

She was there for us when the children got sick and when I felt like my world was crashing. Truthfully, she was one of the best neighbors I ever had. The world could take lessons from her example. People today don't take the time to care. I know what its like to be so blessed with a caring neighbor and a good friend.

"Stempie" was so kind and she needed us as badly as we needed her. She taught me a lot about parenting and cooking and canning. She also grew the most beautiful pansies I had ever seen. When I see a pansy today I think of her very fondly.

Neighborhood

Our girls were growing and would be going to school. They were still struggling with English, Shirley doing much better than Patricia. When they did go to school, the teachers had a hard time understanding them. They had a language of their own. They insisted on being together. As this was an answer for the teachers, they agreed to keep them together. Shirley was the more aggressive of the two. Patricia was quiet, but oh so lovable. To this day, she has a hard time with her h's and several other words that are hard for the French speaking people. When the girls had first learned to speak, it was the French, Chippewa-Cree spoken by their grandparents with whom they lived.

They never lacked for friends. Our house was a meeting place for all the neighborhood children. When the project was built, they also built schools, a theater, a large grocery store, and a drug store. Orchard Heights, a grade school, and Madrona Heights, a junior high school are still in use today. The original stores and theater are no longer in use.

The apartments and all housing were torn down after the war. Lots were sold to private people, real estate agents and new homeowners. We got a face lift, a new look for the drab reminder of the war years. All new houses, taking on the personalities of the new owners.

Pajama Escort

My younger brother Tony was in the service, he enlisted when he was 18. He chose the Navy and when his ship came into the Bremerton port, he spent all his leave time with us. He would spend the night so he could be with the children and have a taste of home life. I missed him, as we were close.

The problem for me was to get Tony back to the ferry so he could get to his ship on time. One time, we had stayed up late and slept in. Tony came and woke me up. I had to hurry, no time to put street clothes on. I rolled up my pajama legs and wore a long rain coat. I took my brother to the Annapolis

ferry. The ferry was in and the road in front of the
dock was jammed with people. I stopped long enough
to let him out and my car went dead. No gas.

Tony wanted to stay and help me but I urged
him on, so he ran to catch the ferry. I was in the way
as people had to go around me, what to do? I was in
night clothes and had no gas tokens. At that time,
the ferry made several runs to and from the
Bremerton dock, loading and unloading the yard
workers. As I got out of the car, my pajamas kept
falling down. Soon a police officer drove up and
offered his help. He asked a passer-by to help him
push my little Ford out of the way. Then he offered
to drive me home. I felt so stupid and embarrassed
to think the neighbors might see me coming home
at that hour with a police officer bringing me home.
Since that time, I never leave the house unless I am
fully clothed. Lesson learned.

**From Left to Right: Brother Tony,
Dorothy (Fred's Wife), Brother Fred**

Brother Fred and Brother Tony

As if the war wasn't enough, life kept on dealing
its usual quantity of sad times. Tony shipped out and
I didn't see him for a long time. He was called back
to Washington State on emergency leave, as our
brother Fred had passed away. At the time of his
death, Fred was married. He was a barber, and drove
school bus part time. He also fathered a son. His son

was only two weeks old when Fred died. His heart had given out.

I left my babies and met my father and a sister, CeCelia and Tony in Davenport, Washington. Fred was buried in Spokane, Washington. After the funeral, we all left for our respective homes. Tony was to catch up with his ship in a California Port. He took a train going south, Dad went east, myself and CeCelia went west.

We settled back into our daily routines. I listened to the news on the radio. There had been a train wreck in Idaho. Some of the people were very injured, had lost their luggage, and some of the injured servicemen did not have I.D. tags. They gave descriptions of some of the men that were critical, and asked for anyone who could possibly provide identifications, to come to Spokane. Aunt Sarah was sure one of the men was Fred's brother Tony. She and Uncle Joe drove to Spokane to make sure. And it was Tony.

He was hurt badly, teeth knocked out, and many other broken limbs and lacerations. He was in the hospital for a long while. When he was well enough, he rejoined his ship somewhere in the South Pacific. I didn't see Tony until the war was over.

Brother Tony and our Father

Mike the Second

The war years also brought their share of blessings.
While living in our house by the side of the road, I
had another boy child. I named him Michael, after
me. I was always called Mike when I was growing up.
He was a beautiful boy child and very welcomed into
the family circle. But of course, all six of my babies
were beautiful, Shirley Rose, Patricia Joann, William
John, Thomas James, Michael Anthony and
Christopher Raymond (he hadn't made his
appearance at this point).

The War is Ended...

August 15, 1945

I had the radio on I was listening to the news and mixing a big batch of bread. "THE WAR IS OVER" the announcer kept repeating. I could hear his emotions spewing over, he was all choked up. He wanted to laugh and cry all in the same breath. I heard whistles blowing, church bells ringing.

My friend drove in and she, too, was all emotional. She said, "Grab the kids and lets go into Bremerton and watch all the festivities." "Gosh Aggie, I can't go, I have a big batch of bread I will have to punch it down and put it in pans." She said, "Bring it along." So, with my four babies and a big batch of dough, we took off for Bremerton. Traffic was bumper to bumper. I guess we thought all the men would be on the ships, just like magic, returning home. It's funny how one's mind can visualize all that's to come, and expecting it to happen all in one moment.

We could not find a parking spot, Aggie drove up and down, people were shouting greetings and laughing and hugging. What a glorious day. I punched

my dough down, several times. I should have left it home
as it soured and just completely refused to rise again.
(It certainly was dough well spent)

Now that the war was over, Joseph got laid off.
He had been hired on as a temporary employee. If
he had gotten in two weeks earlier, he would have
been permanent.

This was the fall and winter of 1945 to 1946—
Joseph worked part time at his mechanic job and
collected unemployment, so we were able to stay in
our little house by the side of the road.

I Was Determined

In the early spring of '46 we headed back to
Montana to visit Joe's parents and help them with all
the chores. My vacation was to clean, paint, cook,
and of course, take care of my family. Joseph got a
job in the schools, painting and doing all the repair
work that was needed to get the buildings back in
shape for the fall school season.

It didn't pay much, but helped to pay our
expenses on our return trip to Port Orchard,
Washington. I kept talking about going home.
Summer was slipping by and I wanted to get my little
girls enrolled in school for the big start of their lives.
In my wildest dreams I could not even think about
staying in Poplar, Montana. I was determined. Joseph
seemed satisfied to stay on the reservation. I wanted
a better life for all of us. Joseph's mother brought all
her forces to bear on him. She begged, pleaded, and
cried. She reminded him he had no job to go back
to. She was a very possessive and a domineering
person. She wanted us to enroll the girls in school so
we could all live together. I could not visualize us all

together under one roof. I went that route once, and once was enough.

Joseph went to work every morning and came home for lunch. I was busy washing and packing. I was leaving. If Joseph wanted to stay, that would be his choice. But I for one, was going to leave with my little brood.

Early this one Friday morning, I got the children up, got them dressed and fed, and loaded the car. I packed a big lunch, and got the children in their seats. They were all small enough to fit in the backseat. My heart was in my throat, I was choking and my stomach was in knots. But I was leaving. Joseph's mother was still crying and begging him, to make me change my mind. So very reluctantly, Joseph got in the car and we were on our way. We did not speak to each other for miles. "No Way" would I change my mind or even consider going back.

The second day on the road, we talked about no job and some of the options. On the brighter side, we had a little house, our health and friends. We had a little savings we might have to use. Things looked much better as time and the miles rolled by. Finally, we got home to Port Orchard. I never thought our little house would look so beautiful. It was mine to rule and to finally have the say over my little ones. For the first time in all my married life, I felt like I was the Mother, and was in complete control and I loved it.

Why do we let our in-laws have so much control? The old adage, "Honor your father and mother" is well and good, but we must also be entitled to raise our children the way we want to. We had values and we had learned from our own upbringing and experiences that changes were in order.

Joseph Goes Job Hunting

Joseph had been a welder in the Bremerton Navy Shipyard. His second job was as a mechanic in a garage. He worked at these two jobs all during the war. When we got back to Port Orchard, he went to see his old employer at the garage. When the war ended, so did many other things. People moved away and jobs were not so plentiful. This man was a friend, he told Joseph he really didn't have that much work, but he would help us out and give him a few days when he could. This would put food on the table.

In the meantime, Joseph submitted applications for any and every job in the Navy Yard. He was finally called to work as a sweeper. He reported to work and was on the job for a couple weeks, when the Leadman from his welding years happened to see him pushing a broom and asked him what he was doing there? Joseph said, "I am feeding my family." They parted without any further conversation. The next day, Joseph was told to report to the welding supervisor. He was given his old job back and his rating. He held that job for 33 years, thanks to this friend and supervisor, and thanks to my Joseph.

Farm Life and New Experiences

If I thought our house was full, overflowing would have been a more apt description. We were seriously thinking of finding bigger quarters. We heard of a farm that was for sale—what a joy that would be, to have some elbow room.

We went to look at this farm—5 plus acres. What a house: massive bed rooms, living room, dining room, even a pantry! The upstairs had a winding staircase, the bedrooms were huge. One bedroom was 18 feet by 26 feet. We used it as a dormitory for all our boys. We had three boys when we moved in. Then there was two other bedrooms upstairs, not quite as large, but very spacious. The closets were not finished and were big enough for bedrooms. Joseph finished them off and made walk-in closets, complete with shelves and racks. The master bedroom downstairs was 18 feet by 22 feet. With a house that big, there was only one bathroom. Yes, we did buy it. It proved to be a good investment and a proper place to raise our family. Michael was barely walking when we moved in.

We sold our little house by the road. If I thought I knew what work was, it was child's play compared to our life on the farm. Everybody worked and we all had to learn to make this farm pay off. First we bought a cow, then some chickens and rabbits. Joseph bought an old tractor with all the attachments needed to work up the ground. Joseph was still working swing shift. This left the daylight hours for him to work around the farm and/or do the remodeling on the house, it was in such disrepair.

The garden was plowed and ready for seed; here is where our dear old friend Stempie came to the rescue. Advice is what I needed. Then too, the orchard needed pruning. We had every kind of fruit tree, from apples, to cherries, to plums (different varieties of them), plus raspberries, boysenberries, strawberries and grapes. The boys learned to milk the cow, put up hay, and all the hundreds of jobs that go with farming.

Michael, our youngest, would go out into the chicken pen and sit on the ground with the chickens and eat the mash out of the feeders. I would see him and pluck him out of there. One day he got away from me and ran out to the chicken pen and the rooster met him and didn't like him butting in on his harem. So the rooster attacked him and took a hunk out of his lower lip. I grabbed him and called the neighbor to watch over the other kids while I took Mike to the doctor for stitches. When Joseph came home he kept wiping Mike's lower lip thinking it was something that shouldn't be there. I hollered at him, "Don't touch his mouth, those are stitches."

"Stitches, how come?"

"That darn Rooster attcked him today."

Joseph went right to the chicken pen and chopped the roosters head off.

Michael also loved to sit down under the tree and eat the plums when they were ripe. His brothers and sisters would go out there in the orchard and pick them off the ground so Mike couldn't get to them. But as soon as I would turn him loose, that little bugger would head for the prune tree. I watched him get a stick and hit the lower branches and the prunes would fall off in droves. He would plunk himself down and eat. I got tired of changing dirty diapers so I would send him out without any panties on. He was going to eat them regardless of what any of us did.

Our girls, being the oldest, were the housekeepers. They learned to bake, cook, and do housework while the boys and I did the chores. Joseph worked two jobs. He would help with the haying, cutting and raking; it was up to us to get it in the barn. This event usually happened around the fourth of July, much to the dismay of all the children we could not go on any picnics because the hay had to come first. It usually rained on the fourth of July, that justified our staying home.

More Work but More Room
Our new farm house on Mt. View Drive

**Left to Right: Top—Patricia, Shirley
Bottom—John, Mary, Michael, Joseph, Tom**

Life Gets Even Busier

We met our neighbors, joined the community club, a garden and farm-oriented club, where we met new people and became members.

During this time I was elected Precinct Committee Woman, a position I held for several years. Our children became involved in Cub Scouts and Girl Scouts. As their mother, I too volunteered to be an active member—as Den Mother, Girl Scout leader and by taking an active part in the PTA.

These were all learning experiences for me. As I look back now, I must have had a lot of ambition. I don't know how I did all that I did. I had a lot of help and support from the family. We had good times and bad, the good outweighing the bad. A sense of humor saw me through many a situation.

I was even able to see the humor in some of the boys' antics. The two older boys, John and Tom, were at the "big hunter" stage, what with five acres at their disposal. They had no guns at that young age, not even a sling shot. They had been promised a 22 caliber when the time came. They, being the true sons of a mother who had done so in her youth, went the route of making their own bows and arrows, and sling shots.

Every day I was busy with farm concerns and other matters. They played in the garage; if I didn't hear any blood curdling screams, I assumed all was well, and the day would end when they came in for homework and then bed.

Every weekend, Joseph was home and there were many jobs to be completed. Every undertaking was a learning project. One weekend, after breakfast, Joseph went out to the garage and came back with a strange look in his eye. I knew something was wrong when he asked if the boys had been working in the garage. He held up what had been a new inner tube, now all cut up, and his pair of work boots, minus the tongues.

What did they know about these mangled items? They said they were sorry, yes they would ask permission to use his stuff the next time, only "Dad, you aren't home when we are." I could relate to this. So often it seemed he really wasn't home when we needed him. It was so hard and intimidating to have to make all the decisions by myself and worry if I had made the right choice.

We had our church, friends and school activities. The two older boys were into baseball. This was uplifting and was so much fun for all of us. They played baseball all through their school years. John continued even when he went to work as an apprentice in the Navy Yard. They had a team composed of men who worked in his shop. They were quite good and won State and drove to Ohio for the finals. They did not win as they were "too pooped to pop" after that long drive. But fun they did have and some good memories. I think that is how I felt most days while we lived on the farm.

Our girls were growing up. The girls, Shirley and Patricia, were teenagers then. Boys with healthy hormones began cluttering up my life. At sixteen, these boys were cocky little roosters who thought they were God's gift to young ladies. This mother thought not.

The girls could not date, so we had a lot of extra girls sleeping over, and, it was okay to have a few of these little roosters over for dancing. The girls would make sandwiches, popcorn, cookies and, we must not forget the Kool-Aid. Curfew was 11:30 p.m. I had quite a reputation as a very strict parent. We kept it that way. Sleepovers were any night of the week, but to have these little imitators of Elvis, with the swivel hips, duck tail haircuts and blue suede shoes, could and would, only be tolerated once a week, on Friday.

1950≠Life Is Getting Better

I got a Babysitter. Our lives on the farm were rolling along quite smoothly. We all had our designated chores and found we could trade off when things become boring or outside activities got in the way—such as getting our neighbor to milk "old bossy" when number one son wanted to turn out for a school function.

It was easier for me to call the boys by numbering them "number one son," "number two son," right down the line until they were all accounted for. Otherwise, I had to name them all before I got the right one. They knew their spot in the right pecking order. Even today, when they call me on the phone, they will say this is "number one son" or "number three son" whichever they are. I got so frustrated when I wanted one boy and had to call them all. I would say "Oh hell, forget it" because by that time I was the one who forgot what I wanted the particular son for.

I realized we were all kept so busy that we had no time for anything like a movie. Our only entertainment was what we made for ourselves. Neighborhood get togethers, kids' ball games, picnics and sometimes we just went out in the orchard and had our lunch. Kids just seemed to pop up out of the grass, always extras to feed, they were always welcome. I didn't bother to count noses we always had enough to eat.

Television, the magic of all things to come, came into our lives. Joseph brought home this big piece of furniture. A beautiful cabinet and this little 9-inch screen of black and white wonderment.

Not to complain, we were the first family in the whole neighborhood to own this bit of luxury. We had a lot of company, come 4 o'clock, when the two stations came alive. Channel Four and Five were the news, then came the Lone Ranger and many more family type programs. Our dear friends Stempie and her Hubby came every evening to watch the news, and then The Lone Ranger. The neighbors always knew where to find their kids—over at the Sayers watching T.V. As time went on, more stations were added, and we had some good family-type programs. Family situations, comedy, westerns, John Wayne movies, just plain good entertainment. It was the best baby sitter I ever had. Joy of Joys they went off the air at 10 o'clock p.m.

The Year is 1953

We had Another Son

All summer we had been busy doing the usual things on a farm, canning, preserving, butchering, putting up hay. I was a little clumsy as I was expecting my sixth child due the latter part of October. It was a difficult pregnancy, but I wanted this baby as I knew it would be my last child. I had corrective surgery to be able to conceive. I wanted another child a boy or girl no matter as long as it was a baby. If it was a girl I wanted to name her Christine, a boy would be named Christopher.

Well, our son arrived on the first of November. Our family was complete. His brothers and sisters were so protective The two girls took over, they did everything, mixed formula and had all of the clothes, diapers, and change of clothes next to my bed as I was a basket case, Joseph was home with me during the day and as soon as the girls came home from school they took over, taking turns at cooking and the care of our little Chris. I was in bed for three weeks. My recovery took well over six months. He was worth it, no baby was ever so loved, The girls would rush in the house the minute they got home from school. If Chris was asleep they would wake him up and play with him and do the necessary changes. He would wake up in such a cheerful manner and was always smiling and so happy. He was so special and he still is.

Michael and Chris

His older brothers would take him on wagon rides, hitching up the family "guard dog" to the little red wagon. This guard dog was a royal pain in the butt. If people came to visit, whether friend or foe, we would have to remove him physically from the doorway. It wasn't because he was such a protector, he was just too lazy to move. Then, we realized he was a chicken thief and killer so we gave him back to the original owner. From that day on this friend completely ignored Joseph when he did see him. Look at the bright side, how many chicken's lives have been saved? Only to be slaughtered for a Sunday dinner. Yes, that's life and death and Sunday dinners.

Dad

My Dad died in November, 1953. I could not go home for his funeral as I had just birthed number four son. I truly loved my Dad and feel like he should be there at the old homestead. When I go back to Dakota I still feel like he has to be there. This is why I think we need to have a closure, to visibly see and participate in the funeral mass and burial.

Welcome Home Tony

It was good to see Tony again. He and a cousin hitchhiked out from Montana and North Dakota. The war had been over for a while. We were all so happy to see them.

As we were still on the farm we had gobs of room and were happy to have family with us. Cousin Bernard stayed with us a few days then went to Bremerton to be with his immediate family. They had both been in this area during war time and liked the rain.

Both the boys went job hunting and both were now veterans. Bernard pursued a career as a cosmetologist, Tony went to work in the Navy Yard. Bernard met this cute little gal who was also studying cosmetology, love blossomed.

Tony came home from work one evening and asked our little Pat who was in the third grade, what her teacher's name was. Patty answered, "Miss Degnan." So Uncle Tony proceeded to ask her all about this teacher. It seems that Miss Degnan's sister, Ardys, was the little cutie that Bernard had his eye on. The boys double-dated and after a period of time, Tony married Miss Degnan and Bernard married

Ardys. They had the first double wedding in our new Catholic Church, First Catholic Church in Port Orchard. They both had large families and have been an asset to the community.

We all had large families and did not get together too often. When the children were smaller it was no problem, but as they all grew up, more space was needed. It was a comfort knowing that they were all around us and we only had to push a few buttons to call and visit or get together an impromptu party.

Farm Life Comes To An End

Life on the farm had to come to an end. All the children, except Chris, went on to pursue other facets of life. Tom and Mike went in the Service. John got married and was an apprentice in the Navy Yard. The girls were both married. Chris was so allergic to hay, we realized it was time to move on.

We found a house on the beach with a lovely view on the bay. Our Chris loved to fish and had his own little pram. He kept us in fresh cod. He soon learned where the deep holes with all the cod were. He would take the neighbor boy out with him. They were real careful and soon I quit worrying about him as long as he was in sight.

This home needed a lot of repair, so Joseph again had to apply his skill with the old hammer and saw. Joseph added a new kitchen, and another bedroom upstairs. We had Shirl's boys most of the time. Oh, how they loved it here on the beach. There was a six years age difference between Chris and our grandson, Tom. They made a rope swing from a tree. On the bank side, they would climb up the slope and hang on the rope for dear life and come swinging way out over our property. Soon all the kids in the neighborhood would be enjoying the thrill of the ride. They were all told they had to have parental permission and that we would not be responsible if they got hurt. Now I could settle down and be domestic.

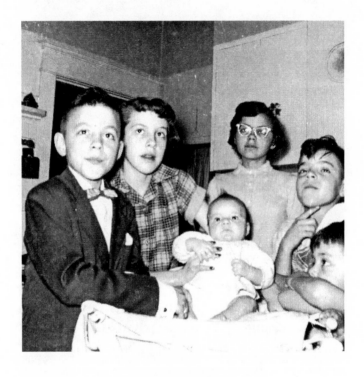

**From Left to Right: John, Shirley,
Patrica, Tom, Michael
Center: Chris**

Shirley and Patrica attending formal dances

Our new home on Beach Drive

At this time, Joseph and I became serious "Rock Hounds." We joined the Kitsap Gem and Mineral Club and met many wonderful people.

On one of our trips back to Montana we went
looking for agates. I found one right on a gravel road,
and we had it cut and made into a ring. That started
us on a hobby that was so relaxing. After digging your
heart out, admiring your find and sharing it with
other members, you could forget all your stress for a
little while. I also learned that I didn't have a corner
on the stress market.

Our newfound friends had also raised families
and we had much in common. Camping and rock
pow wows became a way of life during the summer
months. We would mix business with pleasure.

Pursuing our favorite hobby

Monks and Monastery Wine

Going back to the Dakotas was always so nostalgic.
We would look for rocks, fossils, and anything that
didn't move and had to be dug out. We always
stopped to visit family along the route. One Sunday
we were driving south to visit Sister Gen and her
husband, Lyle, who lived in Hebron, North Dakota.
The road seemed endless. There were no homes,
just large farms. Everything was so green and trees

were in full blossom—cottonwoods, lilacs, wild roses. The whole countryside looked so serene, and majestic.

I looked at Joseph and said, "This is a day we should be in church. You know Joe, it is Sunday." We kept driving and soon I spied a sign that said, "Russian Orthodox Catholic Church." I said, "Look, Joe. There is a Catholic church. Let's stop and go to Mass." We pulled in the parking lot, and there was plenty of room to turn the fifth wheeler around with no problem. We got out of the truck and went into the church.

How strange. The men were seated on the right side and the women on the left. The children were seated in the front pews. We didn't know what to do. Joseph was all for exiting—real fast. I casually held his arm and we proceeded to find a vacant pew way down in front with the children.

It turns out these were Russians from the old country. They did not look directly at us. As we sat there, we could feel all those eyes on us, even though they didn't turn their heads. Joseph was still uneasy, but I told him that this was God's house and I was sure it would be all right. They say, "When in Rome do as the Romans do." So, we watched for clues.

Soon the mass started, it was sung in the Russian language. The prayers were said in English. There was no organ, only a blending of voices. It was the most beautiful singing I had ever heard. I was so happy we stopped and I could hardly wait to speak to the "Father" and convey my feelings. I could not keep my eyes off the beautiful gold icons.

When it came time for communion, I got a good grip on my husband's arm and went up to the

communion rail with our peers. It was a most unusual
way to receive. Little tiny cone-shaped dippers were
filled with wine and a small cube of bread was
dropped in the dipper. You stuck out your tongue
and the sacred host and wine was placed on your
tongue. All too soon the service came to an end.

The Father stood out on the front steps, I thought
to greet all his flock. But not a word was said—not
even a handshake. We left feeling much better for
having gone to Mass and to hear that heavenly singing.
It was well worth the stop. We were quiet for a few
miles, both of us in deep thought. So much so that
we missed our turn off, and soon found ourselves
almost back in Montana. My fault again. No harm
done. We just kept on going and stopped in to see
Teddy Roosevelt Park, and another good place to
turn around.

After that little fluke we kept going east and soon
saw the sign, Hebron. We turned off the freeway and
soon arrived at my little sister Gen's home. After our
greetings were over, I expounded on our church
episode. I told them I was changing over from Roman
Catholic to the Russian Orthodox. It turns out we
had done something that they had never done. They
were curious about this church, and the people. My
brother-in-law said this was a very tight community
and they did not associate with any of the natives.
They were hard working people, God and family
came first.

During our visit we took in the sights of museums
and two Indian reservations. Then we drove to
Richardton and the Assumption Abbey, now almost
deserted, with only a few Monks living on the
premises as caretakers. In 1899, Abbot Wehrle moved
the priory from the shores of Devils Lake, North
Dakota, to keep in touch with the German, Russian

and Hungarian immigrants who settled in that area. The Russian influence remains today. These people farmed and helped to settle the area.

At one time it was a beautiful monastery with hundreds of monks. They were there as spiritual advisers, teachers (grades 1-8) and to pray, pray, pray. Their lives were dedicated to prayer. They were silent and no talking was allowed, and only at specified times.

They farmed hundreds of acres, and planted a vineyard raising different kinds of grapes. They made their own sacramental wines. Soon these wines became known throughout the Diocese, so they supplied all the communion wine for the churches. They also sold to the public. My sis asked the little monk if they still had the winery. "Yes," he said, but they did not produce the volume that they used to. "Now days" he said, "So few people drive off the freeway, unless they have heard about them." We toured the Abbey from top to bottom. Most interesting was the Native American Indian Museum. Everything was authentic—from clothing to teepees, and old kitchenware that looked better than what we were used to while growing up.

The monks had special sides of the alter where they knelt while saying their prayers. The floor was so well worn, I wondered how callused their knees were.

The Father who took us on this tour was such a happy little fellow, he asked us if we would like to see the wine cellar and do a little tasting. Gen looked at me I looked at her as if to say, "We thought you'd never ask." We followed the little padre down long hall ways, down stairs. In the dark, we reached a door at the end of the hall where he opened a big heavy door and we entered. Padre flipped the light switch on and we were in the inner sanctuary. It smelled dank and musty. There was a bar with wine glasses on the shelf. Padre removed five glasses, wiped them off and went to the wine rack, where he read the label and the date. He picked one bottle up and proceeded to open it. He told us it might not be good, he would have to try it first. He explained that sometimes wine will revert back to the vinegar state. He then reached for the crackers. With a flourish that could not be duplicated by any noted actor, he poured a little wine in his glass, rolled it around and took a sip. Then he rolled his eyes heavenward and we looked on in wonderment, Was it or wasn't it? Another sip, eyes again looking heavenward. He said, "Sebou, Sebou." "So good, so good." He explained that you took a bite of cracker between each sample. Needless to say we bought a bottle of this and a bottle of that.

Our visit with Gen and Lyle was so rewarding. We had brought some fresh salmon and oysters from Washington. Gen invited her dear friends over for a barbecue and the big event was the fresh sea food. And our BIG purchase when we visited the Abbey.

Lyle fired up the barbecue, and we gals cooked the salmon and oysters, all the while enjoying the fruit of the vine. Gen's friends came and we had an evening to remember.

Mama's Later Years

Mama stayed in Dakota after Dad died in 1953 and traveled from state to state wherever her children lived. Whenever one of us needed her to come and help us out she was there for us. There were five of us left and we kept her busy, helping with all her grandchildren.

Mama decided to make her permanent home here in Washington State. She moved to our great state in 1968 and lived with Brother Tony for some time. Tony helped her get her own apartment. She was a very happy camper from then on and was able to do her own housekeeping and shopping. She made a lot of friends, through her church and her neighbors. As the years piled up, she seemed to be ageless. She was young at heart and truly was the matriarch.

Mama's descendants numbered around one hundred. She was the focal point of all our gatherings. Every holiday and every birthday the whole clan would get together. The most important days were Christmas and her birthday. We made a big event out of her birthday. She loved to get gifts and no one forgot her. These two days were hers. This is where everybody got together. With so many of us Mama never lacked for an invitation from other family members.

I am so happy we were able to do these things for her as her life was one of poverty and she had to go without all the years she was raising us kids. She loved all her grandchildren and great grands not equally as I have learned, since I am also now a great grandmother. Some have special little traits and are more in tune with you. Some are more thoughtful, more lovable. Need I say more? We as grandparents should treat them all alike, and I'm sure we all try to.

As Mama got older she required more help from all of us. She lived in Bremerton, we lived in Port Orchard. We were taking her to doctors, shopping, cleaning her house and doing her laundry. Finally,

Mama didn't have to do anything but cook, and this she loved to do.

She was in her 90's when we realized she couldn't see. We took her to numerous optometrists and learned she was going blind. At this point, she only had peripheral vision and nothing could be done. She would always be able to see a gray mist and shadows.

Mama loved to fly and all her trips were by air. Her last trip was to North Dakota to attend a grandson's wedding. While back in North Dakota she had a mild stroke and was in the hospital. It was then we learned she was legally blind and would not be able to live alone.

Our youngest sister, Gen, came back to Washington with her. We needed Gen to help us get Mama transferred to a nursing home. We knew it wouldn't be easy. Mama loved her little apartment. For the first time in her life, she had things a lot handier and was her own boss. This was a very traumatic move for all of us.

Mama made great progress. She did not let her blindness get in her way. She was a care giver, even in the nursing home. Every night she would make the rounds, knocking on the doors and calling out the patient's name, going in and asking, "Are you all right, Katy? Do you need anything? Are you warm enough?" With this last question, she would feel her way along the foot of the bed and proceed to tuck them in. Then she would pat on down to the next room, her little slippers flop, flop, flopping down the hallway. Saying her "good nights" and "God bless you" to all her peers. Only then could Mama get her toilette done and go to bed, rosary in hand and trust in the good

Lord to see her through the night. With such a large family, Mama prayed for all of us. She always had her rosary in her pocket. If you saw her resting, with eyes closed, no she wasn't sleeping. She was praying for her family. I miss her so much.

Only now do I understand some of the hardships and the sacrifices she made for all of us. Only now do I wish I could undo some of the things I did that caused her so much heartache.

Mama was a psychic, a gift she did not care to have. She kept it well hidden as she felt it would just be one more thing to add to her grief. People would not understand. People called it witchcraft, or being possessed by the Devil. The term psychic was not part of her language. You see, my Mama was a real "metis." Her mother and dad were from Canada, both were half-Chippewa Indian and half-French. Metis means "We of the half bloods."

Josephs fishing paid off—45lb salmon
Mama and Mary

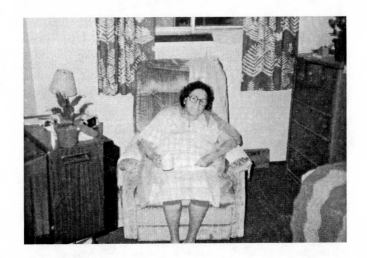

Mama at Port Orchard Care Center

Both of Mama's parents were raised in Canada, however, Mooshum (grandfather) was born in the area of Green Bush, Minnesota. Kookum (grandmother) was raised in Canada by the nuns from the Ursuline Order of Sisters. As a young boy growing up alone in his village in Minnesota, Mooshum was befriended by a missionary priest who traveled from one village to another, converting the natives. This priest took Mooshum with him, and made a Catholic and altar boy out of him. They traveled all over the territory, by horse and buggy, ending up in Canada, which is now Manitoba Province. This priest had a little altar that they used when saying mass. It was very easy to put up in a hurry and is a wonderful piece of art.

There were large bands of Objibwa (Chippewa) and many French fur traders. Of course, this entire area was populated by the French. This is where my grandparents had their beginnings.

Mama did not know anything about her parents, how they met or when they got married. Her mother's maiden name was Martin. She knew they were married in Canada. They had one son and when he was three years old, they packed up all their belongings in a wagon pulled by a team of horses and headed for the Dakotas. Mooshum was given the little portable altar. It was a part of their lives and Mama inherited it. She passed it down to brother Tony. To this day it has a place of honor in Tony and Fern's bedroom. If it could talk, I'm sure it would have wonderful stories to tell.

When Mama's parents were en route

somewhere near White Earth, North Dakota,
Kookum, who was quite pregnant, went into labor.
Mooshum made camp none too soon as my Mama
made her appearance the 31st day in May of 1893.
As soon as Kookum regained her strength, they
continued on and settled along the Missouri River
close to what is now the Montana and Dakota line.

Many Metis from Canada also migrated to this
area and it soon became populated with half-
bloods. As time went on, they began to mix a little
English with French and Chippewa. They called
themselves "Metchi"or "Mitchiff."

When I was growing up and we heard other
people call us these names, we thought it was
derogatory and a put down. Today, when a Metis
goes to Canada, they are told they speak a bastard
French. The French spoken in Canada is not the
same as the French spoken in France. This leaves
us to realize that all people, no matter how mixed
up in race, will bring a little of each nationality into
play. Language will change with each generation.

My Mama was a very important part of my time. I
wish I would have taken more time to know her as a
mother and friend instead of giving up my time to
lesser projects. Or, if I could relive those times and
learn from her. Her time was also all tied up with the
mundane talks of feeding and clothing eleven
children. All this took place during the dust bowl
and the great depression era, late 1920 to the 1930's.
There was no time for small talk.

I Go Back to School

Now that I had my family raised, and they have pursued their own careers, got married, gone into the service, etc. I could concentrate on my own education. I also became a grandmother. This I love.

In 1970, when I was in my 50s, I went back to school to get my G.E. D. I talked about education to my family—"You must get a good education." Now was the time for me to set a good example. I did what I set out to do. I got my certificate, having passed the equivalency test. Now what was I going to do with this newly acquired document that I so proudly hung on my wall?

A very dear friend of mine who worked for the school system as a secretary usually stopped in for a cup of coffee and some small talk. One day her talk was about a new program that was going to be implemented in our district, and the focus was going to be on Indian education. She knew my background as I am part Native American and felt I should apply for the job, as they only wanted people who were Native American.

Our Indian children were not getting the

education that had been promised in one of over 600 Treaties that were made and not honored.

You give us your land, we will educate your children, take care of all medical needs, build you hospitals. You will have no worries. Yes, these buildings were built. Huge boarding schools, all staffed by white people. If our people had any self esteem, it was soon lost. They lost their identity, and their culture. The elders could see the importance of teaching their children the three "R's." They also knew that these kids needed someone they could identify with, to give them encouragement, to make them proud of who they were. The needed the same opportunities as our white brothers.

I could relate, as I was sent away to a Bureau of Indian Affairs Boarding school, which was staffed by white personnel. They didn't have a clue on how to handle these young "savages." I can't remember a single one of our instructors ever looking at me as a person, or even trying to find out what I was like. I cried real tears, I bled when I was cut, I loved my family. I was a human being. There was only one Matron who realized how lonely my roommate and I were. Most of the students had some money to go to a movie on weekends. We didn't have any money, and this matron would, out of kindness, invite us to her quarters and make us popcorn and talk to us as people. She never realized that we thought she was as close to a Saint as any mortal could be. When I think of my boarding school days, she is the only good memory that comes to my mind, with much love.

I want to relate a true story about a young Indian boy. He was sitting at his desk listening to the teacher, head down and very intent on every word. He did not hear her come alongside him. She called out his name and he did not look up. She grabbed his hair and pulled his head back and said, "Look at me when I talk to you." He did not make eye contact, because in his culture it is disrespectful to look another being in the eyes, the eyes being the mirror of the soul. In his culture, he was being respectful. You do not look into anyone's soul. He did not even try to explain to the teacher. She would not have understood. The distance between the two cultures is like a deep chasm.

I went to work for the School District as an Indian Aide. Monies had been granted only after a group of Indian parents converged on the White House in Washington D.C. and insisted the government honor this very important Treaty right. Indian elders from almost all of the reservations went in a group to make their wishes known.

Our first order of business was to take a census. How many Indian people do we have here? There are reservations all around us, but we are dealing with off-reservation Indians. People who came west to work in the factories and the shipyards. Our work was cut out for us, counting little Indian noses. "One little, two little, three little Indians." A little humor filling out forms. Are you registered in a tribe? Where is your tribe located? What is the name of your tribe? What degree of blood do you have? On and on.

What with all the nose counting, those of us who were hired had to go to school also, to learn about all the other cultural issues. We would work four days and go to Seattle one day a week, and then take one week of lessons at the University of Washington. I was so fascinated with the subject matter. I also learned more about my own culture. I now know where I came from. We did not talk about our heritage at home, and our parents did not enlighten us. We were looked down upon. I made up my mind I would not let my children go through the torment of discrimination, better they not know. Wrong. More on that later. I had much to learn.

Our supervisor and head of the program had specialists from different reservations come and teach us about their culture. Basketry, foods, botany, song and dance, the drum, Indian medicines, the hunters, the root gatherers, etc. Before I became enlightened, I too, thought all Indians were alike. I only knew of my tribe and the Sioux and Assiniboin, the Plains and Plateau peoples.

Here on the west coast and into Alaska are the totem pole carvers, whale hunters, fishermen. So much to learn. I was trying to soak it all up like a sponge. I especially enjoyed the classes that were taught by an honest-to-goodness chief, Lame Deer, "Seeker of Visions," a prophet and medicine man. I learned so much and could have spent the rest of my days learning from him. He has since passed away.

One of the classes we took was an "in service," on song and dance. The music was so rhythmic. You actually began to feel the horse, or any one of the animals that were incorporated into the songs. You could feel and hear the horses, the beat of their hooves, feel the wind in your hair, your own heart beating its own rhythm.

These classes were all in the evening and all too soon would come to an end. We would take a break about mid way though and get acquainted with the other students and our instructor. One time I was talking to this nice Indian man and I was trying to figure out where I'd seen or heard him before. We talked about boarding school days, and were surprised to learn we had both gone to the same school. He was a senior, while I was a junior.

I related my first experience after our arrival. A bus load of us from Montana, North and South Dakota, Wisconsin and other distant states arrived on the same day. All the boys and girls were in attendance in the Auditorium, hearing about the whole operation and what we could do and what we couldn't do. The superintendent then called this young man on stage to sing the "Indian Love Song." It was so beautiful. I have never heard it sung without thinking about this young man and what a gorgeous voice he had. I often wondered who he was, and if he had done anything with his talent. I expressed these things to my Instructor. He straightened up to appear taller and with so much pride, he said, "That was me!" My God, this old man. It couldn't be, but now I knew. I must have appeared to him also as a doddering elderly woman. We did some more visiting and soon it was time to resume our studies. And relive old times and more memories at our next session.

In the meantime, we all made our own drums and could then dance to our own beat. We also made our own carving tools. All of these lessons were passed on to our students.

I finished my education and was certified as an Indian Cultural Specialist. I also earned an Associate Arts Degree in Early Childhood Education from Highline Community College. The degree as Indian Education Specialist was issued to us by Emmet Oliver, who was Superintendent of Indian Affairs in Olympia. That was a proud day for me. Two of my closest friends came to my house to congratulate me on my achievement.

You may wonder why my degree was in Early

Childhood Education. After, all I had already raised
eleven children. I learned that we were to focus on
the primary years, though we worked with grades K-
12.

Teaching and Care Giving

I had my degree and loved my job. My first
assignment was in a junior high school. Six hundred
live bodies, and I mean live. I did not realize the whole
world was crazy or was it, because I had not been around
teenage people since mine were out of the nest.

This period involved drugs, excessive smoking,
foul language, and my little 7th graders were into
snuff. They were only trying to imitate their peers.
My principal was a very understanding man. The kids
did not get away with anything. He was fair and they
saw how caring he was. He ran a tight ship and we
were all the better for it.

I was walking down the hall going to my office
when the principal came abreast. At the same time
one of my students came by. This student was very
small for his age and tried so hard to fit in with all
the other big wheels. As he tried to squeeze by, the
Principal said, "Well, hello there" and gave the
student a hefty pat on the back. The student gulped
and swallowed, and went on his way to class. The
principal told me "Now, you watch. In less than an
hour, we will have one sick little boy. He ingested his
whole wad of snuff." True to his word, this little
student was sent to the office and taken home one
sick little puppy.

I very fondly called this student my little banty
rooster. He was so cocky, what he lacked in size he
made up for in his banter. He never missed any of

the dances. He asked all the girls to dance, even the friendly giants. They never turned him down. I didn't see him for several years, and when I did he was as happy to see me as I was to see him. He graduated from high school and went to work for Taco Bell as the manager. So my little "banty" was well on the road to success. And he proved to me that honest work was not beneath him. Jobs were as scarce then as they are now. I wish him well.

I worked for thirteen years, first at a junior high. Our funding was cut every year to where it was impossible to do a first rate job with the children. I ended up in an elementary school. It was so rewarding to be able to get through to these kids. A one on one was the best way to go. Soon we had no funding at all. Today, it is a pitiful excuse of a program. One person is in charge of all the Indian kids in the district. About all she can do is keep a count so the district will get some moneys. Like all Bureau of Indian Affairs "deals" with the Indians, none of them last very long.

Now with the casinos in the offing, the Native Americans are making a better life for themselves, plus they are able to go to school for higher education. They are also taking care of the elders, and life is much better in the long run. But like all people they, too, can swindle, wheel and deal. They had good teachers. The good outweighs the bad when you consider the rough time they had in days gone by.

Our First Sixty Years

WE CELEBRATE OUR FIRST SIXTY YEARS
JULY *30, 1938*-JULY *30, 1998*

O ur family put all their talents together and whipped up a wonderful outdoor celebration for our 60th Anniversary. This was held at the home of our daughter and son in-law, Pat and Mel Yingling, at Lake Land Village in Allyn, Washington. Immediate family members alone made for a large group, plus all our close friends. Truly a day to be remembered through displayed pictures that depicted our life together. We even got a sixtieth anniversary card from President Clinton and Hilary.

Food and refreshments were plentiful, if you did not get enough to eat or drink it was your own fault. Visiting with old friends and family, was the highlight of our day. Watching the great grandchildren jumping off the pier and the big splash that they made when they hit the water brought back memories of my own childhood. Living by the lake worried our mother as my brother and sisters practically lived in the water on those hellish hot summer days in the Dakotas. Also, watching the prim little teenagers at our party made me realize that I don't want to know what's ahead for these innocent young people. I can only pray all goes well for them. Now they are canoeing, pairing off with a favorite cousin to talk. At this age, you don't say visit, you hang out.

We have met a couple new great grand children from out of state. This brings a total of 11 grandchildren and 15 great great grandchildren. We really have a beautiful tribe of varied cultures. You might say we have a little United Nations all our own.

What a wonderful day it was, friends and family came to honor us and show their love. We spent time reliving past good and bad times over the sixty years. It doesn't seem as that length of time has passed. The day went by so fast not enough time to visit and (hang out) with all the friends and relatives. Next year God willing.

As the families gathered up children, swim wear, odds and ends of clothing, sorting out pots and bowls that held all those delicious concoctions getting ready to go to their respective homes. A feeling of sadness grips me for a few moments, I shrug it off, why let such a happy occasion be spoiled. No I will not let it.

Joseph and I came home and talked about our lives together, our families, and their families with all the caring and sharing we were content with the feeling of being so loved by all. We especially appreciated the tribute, written by our son Mike, about our 60 years together expressing the thoughts and sentiments of all our children.

> Seems like only yesterday some say, when
> they were wed.
> A young and comely couple, both mid-
> western bred.

Her given name was Mary, and most folks
called him Joe,
They spoke the vows in '38 and let the
record show.
Through thick and thin and in between,
they've risen to the call,
To honor God and all their kin, in fact, to
honor all.
Sixty years is quite a feat, just think how
many days.
They lived, they loved, they cried, they
fought,
but always found the ways,
To raise their kids and show their love,
and lend a helping hand.
To make us proud, to know our roots, to
keep us in the "band",
We thank both of you for all you've done,
we know thats been tough.
A thank you from your little "tribe", just
doesn't seem enough!
We say congratulations, on this amazing
day.
Lets celebrate your 60 years and in one
voice all say;

HAPPY ANNIVERSARY MOM AND DAD
We love you!
Pat   Chris   Michael   Thomas   John

We were into the month of August, we had
purchased a mini motor home in March and did not
get to use it as my health was in question. We decided
to go to the ocean and it took me two weeks to get this
little dude packed up. I was down sizing trying to pack

the most necessary things. This little bugger just would not hold all the things I thought we needed that was in the fifth wheeler we sold.

Finally, all the things packed with room enough for food we decided to go to Seaside, Oregon over Labor Day weekend. We looked forward to relaxing and searching the beach for shells and maybe finding some agates to add to our collection. We loved the smell of the sea, with its rotting clams left half eaten by those screaming scavengers the gulls. There were so many things to do and see when camping by the ocean. Joseph and I had many happy times waiting for the crab boats to come in and be able to purchase crab off the boats. Then go back to camp for a feast while washing the crab down with a cold can of beer. We also like to watch the kite flyers and people bargain with the street venders. We looked forward to many more camping trips especially on the ocean.

Little did I know that this would never come to be. My world lost its focus on September 8, 1998. Joesph passed away gracefully while sitting in his chair overlooking the bay, the water and view he loved so much. His parting left a tremendous void, most certainly in me, still felt to this day. As time begins to clear away the pain, inner voices begin to reassure me that Joseph knows what is in my heart. His presence in my life transcends words, as does my reverence for the way he conducted his role as father and role model to our children. We all miss his laugh, his effortless smile, his bottomless desire to make our lives better . . . he was the best of the best. I know this, I think he knows this now too.

Our favorite Hats

25th Wedding Anniversary

40th Wedding Anniversary

50th Wedding Anniversary

60th Wedding Anniversary
Standing: Left to Right—John, Pat, Mike, Tom
Sitting—Mary and Joe

Grandchildren and Great Grandchildren
Left to Right: Justin (great), Tommy holding Tessa (grand),
Mary holding Mari and Katie (greats), Jennifer (grand),
and Melissa (grand)

Postscript

THE LIFE STORY OF OUR FIRST BORN

THE LIFE AND STORY OF OUR
FIRST BORN

SHIRLEY ROSE SAYERS
Born April 22, 1939
Died March 8, 1977, at age 38.

This was to be a wonderful experience. I always wanted to be a mother. When I was a child I injured my spine. This happened when we were playing on a tire swing. Oh what fun it was to wind the swing as tight as it would go, then to release it and go spinning. Well, I went spinning, the rope broke and I landed on a rock right on my tail bone crushing the two end vertebrae. As a result of this accident my whole pelvic bone area was misaligned and I grew up with this deformity.

We were not close to any large city nor did we have access to any doctors. Mama used all her herbal remedies, poultices, etc. I remember I couldn't sit. I had a huge abscess, a high fever, and I was a pretty miserable little critter. A neighbor came to the rescue. He insisted I be taken to the nearest hospital—he even made arrangements to have another neighbor drive us to the city. After a few days I was discharged. I did not know that I was in such bad shape. Nor did I realize the impact this injury would have on my birthing process.

In those days people did not have much choice. We were living on the Fort Peck Indian Reservation, and our first born was to be born in the Government Hospital. I was so happy and looking forward to having this baby. Finally, I went into labor. Hours passed, there was no doctor, only a practical nurse, and she was assisted by another helper. After three days of the most intense pain I have ever had, I prayed to die to rid myself of this horrible pain. But, God must have had other plans for me. I pushed and pushed, I passed out, and finally Shirley was born. She was so beautiful. So worth all the pain. She weighed over 8 lbs. I had no medication, not even an aspirin. I was torn beyond belief and no repair work was ever done.

I could not raise my head, lift my arms or even feed myself. Joseph's aunt was the cook in the hospital. She came in the ward and helped me whenever she could. She would give me a bath and help me go to the bathroom. I was scared out of my mind and so weak I could not move too fast. Every time I went to the bathroom, I had to go through a large ward. All the beds were filled with full blooded Sioux and Assiniboin women. They would strike at me with their canes and tell me I wasn't wanted there. I was not a Sioux. "Get out" they would say. I could not get away from their taunting and hitting at me. My bed was in a sun porch which had doors which could be closed. This porch was actually the maternity ward. All the other young Indian girls gave birth and within a few hours, usually no more than twenty four, they and their little papooses would be on the way home.

I was in the hospital for two and a half weeks. I needed a lot of help and advice. What did I know about the care of a baby and how to take care of myself? I had three more babies in that hospital. All were very difficult births. My last two were born here in Bremerton. It was then I learned the reason why I had such a hard time. My babies would get stuck in the cavity of my pelvic bone. My Doctor was surprised that I lived through the four deliveries. He said they should have all been cesarean section. However, the babies came. I would go through it all again. I love them all so much.

My in-laws moved from Medicine Lake, Montana and moved in with us in Poplar. This little girl was the first grandchild for them. They had lost a daughter two years before our Shirley was born, so to them she was a replacement of their Rosalie. We gave our baby the middle name of Rose. I also "lost" my baby in a way because Grandma took over, she rocked and spoiled her like you wouldn't believe. I was too busy having more babies and trying to keep up with the work. Like I said, no roof is big enough for two women. I was not aware of the complete control I was under. Grandma did not pay any attention to the other children—Shirley was hers.

Now I had three babies, two in diapers and two still on bottles. And Shirley was a toddler. I resented all the attention Grandma was giving to Shirley. I think I even resented my first born. God forgive me, writing this has made me realize my feelings for the first time.

As Shirley grew she would tell me that I did not love her, only Grandma did. I did not stop to smell the roses. I didn't know what else her Grandmother told her. Not until many years later.

Not to be unkind, but I realize now, Grandma's world was pretty small. She did not speak English very well and her world revolved around her granddaughter.

When she became a grandmother at age 49 she took to her rocking chair, only to stir when people came to play pinochle, or when Grandpa rattled the fishing poles. She loved to fish in the Missouri River, catching mostly bull heads, and shiners.

Thank God more grandchildren came along. Soon she had grandchildren from her daughter Ann. We with our little brood were living in the state of Washington. We would go back to visit every summer. My vacation???

Ann and her family made their home with them, so grandmother was in her glory. Shirley was very attached to her grandmother. Shirley's sister, Pat, was so very different. She was so cool and calm, and Shirley could and would talk her into doing her work as well as her own. Pat never seemed to get angry. When they were in high school, Shirley would send Pat home on the first bus, with orders to clean up their room, and get supper started.

Shirley would bring her friends home to spend the night. She never bothered to call to ask. She knew that it would be O.K. The house was big, I was happy to have their friends stay over, I knew where they were then. We had lots of sleepovers.

The girls and their friends were spreading their wings. Testing the waters, teenagers you know, boys were very much a part of the landscape. Most all of their activities were home based. We discussed the do's and don'ts of dating, when, and where, and with whom. We decided that there is safety in numbers, so when they dated they would double date or even triple date. Curfew was before the clock chimed midnight when they must be in the house and ready for bed. It was the hour their Dad got home from work. They knew Dad would be very upset and angry if they weren't home.

High school was fun, the girls dated a lot. It was exciting for me as I did not experience the proms, and all the pomp and primping that they did. Clothes were exchanged with all their friends which added to the excitement of the times.

My worries started when our Shirley started going steady at the age of 16. The love of her life was a year older than she, he was a good kid, had his own car and a job. I did not feel they should be going steady at this age. What does a Mother know?

Frank became a fixture in our home. As soon as he got off work he would come to our house. He was just like one of the family, we fed him and made sure he did not interfere with the girls work. Sometimes I would have to tell him to go home. They dated and were together too much. Weeknights he had to be gone by nine o'clock. Shirley's grades went down, but she was so in love. We sent her to Oregon to school hoping to break them up. We told her if she still felt this way about Frank when she graduated we would go along with her plans.

Sending her away to school did not help one bit. Frank was on his way to get her when we decided to bring her home and do what we could. She was happy to be home and life went on about the same with them and their romance, with one exception—

Shirley quit school in April in her junior year. She wanted to try beauty school, so I took her to sign her up and hoped this would be the answer. I had to drive her to beauty school every morning and Frank would pick her up after school. This seemed to be a good working arrangement. She liked the work and her instructors said she was a natural. When she'd get home we all got haircuts, perms and so on. Shirley seemed happy and was more like herself.

When her instructor called to find out where she was, then I started to worry. She would not call us and I did not know where she was. I would call around and none of her friends knew anything. Her sister Pat was in her senior year and they did not see too much of each other, only at night.

Then one night, Shirley did not come home at all. When her dad came home from swing shift he found me a basket case. In the morning, I called Frank's mom and did not get any answer. I waited by the phone all day, not knowing if she was O.K. or not. It was devastating.

About five o'clock the next day she arrived home. Frank drove her, but he did not come in the house. Pat was home from school and our little Shirley was on the defensive side. She very bluntly told me that she and Frank got married! They drove to Aberdeen, Washington to get married and Frank's mother went with them, since he was not of legal age. Shirley had just turned 18.

She went up to her room and packed a few of her belongings and said they would be staying at his parents place for a while, but that she would keep in touch. The dam burst and I cried so hard. I still don't know if it was from relief that she was

O.K. or a pile-up of all the ups and downs, since all my hopes for her seemed gone. I knew what it was like to be married so young and I wanted to shield both my girls from that. I wanted them to have all the good things, education, good job and then marriage and babies.

Pat put her arms around me to comfort me, and she said, "Mom, I will never do anything to hurt you like you are hurting now." And she never has.

Pat graduated and went to work in Seattle along with one of her classmates. She did not like the hustle and bustle of the city, and I was so relieved when she moved back home and got a job locally. She married and moved to Seattle, but soon they moved back to Port Orchard. Pat always wanted a big family but had to be content with the one little boy she birthed.

On the other hand, Shirley was a duplicate of me. She gave birth to four boys in five years, big babies. They were all healthy but they took a lot of zip out of their little mama. Shirley was so scared, and nervous she did not know what to expect before her first baby was born. I would not tell her the horror stories of her birth and the rest of my babies' births, and I did not know any other way. I told her not to be afraid that the doctors had more modern methods and had medicine for pain. God gave us the ability to forget any and all pain from childbirth. I told her that your love for your baby would wipe out all the hurt.

From left to right: Uncle Mike, Tom, Ron, Mark, Shirley

Her doctor was also a family friend. He prescribed a tranquilizer for her and told her that she was such a nervous person, that she would have to take them all her life. This was the start of a nightmare that I wish never happened. She developed a fixation that she had to have the pills because, "Doctor said so." Drugs were becoming a part of our culture.

They rented a house next door to our farm. It was much handier for me to just run over to help her with her boys. Her sister Pat was a wonderful sitter, along with all her brothers. Frank was working, he delivered milk and also tried his hand at delivering bread. He finally ended up working as an auto body man. His bread and milk routes kept him away from home much longer than if he were on a 9 to 5 schedule. Leaving Shirley and her boys alone, and she just couldn't cope. She started taking more and more tranquilizers. To see your little girl so "rummy" and not able to help her see the horror of what these pills were doing to her, was a nightmare of the worst kind. The more babies she had the more dependent she became.

We, as her parents, tried to help them find more meaning in their lives. We purchased an old rundown house on a 5 acre piece of land. It was a family venture. The house was remodeled, and everybody pitched in. The end results were well worth the effort. It became a three bedroom home with 2 bedrooms upstairs. We sold it to the kids with no money down and a small stipend every month, hoping this would give them an incentive to have a home of their own. It just made more work for me as I was now taking care of two families. Running back and forth and seeing my little Shirley was not getting the help she needed. Her doctors cut out all her medication, but she was getting pills from other sources.

Back Row: Shirley's sons (Tom, Ron, Mark, Tony)
Front Row: Cousins (Danny and Kevin)

We sent her to counselors and had her evaluated in mental clinics. They all told us that she was very normal and had a very high IQ. She tried so hard to stay off pills. She substituted vodka for them. She seemed real normal at times and her happy little self, Then all too soon she would be right down in the depths of hell, her guilt would overwhelm her, and she would resort to drink.

We would talk and pray together. Holding her in my arms she would tell me she didn't know why she did this or why prayers did not help. I had no answers then and I have no answers now. Her boys were all in school. Still no help. She would have her good days and her bad days. She loved her boys, and was so proud of them. They all played baseball in Little League, but she would go to the games while under the influence of the pills and alcohol. These little boys held their heads up and went through all the motions. I'm not sure if she realized the extent of the damage that she was inflicting on them, she just could not see the harm being done.

Pat, a friend, and I went to consult with Shirley's Doctor. We asked about having Shirley committed to a mental hospital. He suggested we try a new facility that had opened up in the area. It dealt with alcohol abuse and he seemed to think it may help, as we were dealing with an addiction. It was worth a try, so with Frank's consent we took Shirley to this facility. The patients there all seemed so friendly and so very normal. Maybe this is what we were praying for: We could not visit for two weeks. We knew in our hearts she would be drug-free these two weeks, hopefully it would be a lasting thing.

She was such a joy to be around when she was our Shirley. It was such a relief to be able to go to bed and get a good sleep without worrying for these two weeks.

We visited when we could, she seemed so relaxed and was having a good time. We thought that maybe this would work.

Two weeks went by so quickly. Shirley went home, that is, to her home. They moved from the little house we had prepared for them because Shirley felt it was too far from town. With the help of a realtor friend, they found a house one block from the school and practically on the Little League ball field and purchased it. This turned out to be an ideal location, since the boys were always at the ball field. We all did everything we could to help.

My mother was living out here and I had a duty to help her too. I was stretched as far as I could be and still was numb. I tried to keep some semblance of a normal life.

Unfortunately, Shirley went back to her old ways.

She couldn't cope with the stress of raising four
robust boys. Again, we went to the doctor. We asked,
"Can't we commit her? She is killing herself and we
don't know where she is half the time or who she is
with." The Doctor said we would have to take her to
a judge and have her committed through the courts.
So my friend, my Pat, and I went to court and had
Shirley committed. By this time, she was so out of it
she didn't know where she was and she did not put
up any resistance. We drove to Tacoma through a
heavy rain, found the hospital and went to
admittance to sign the necessary papers. The nurse
wanted us to accompany her to her room.

Shirley came out of her fog and when we went
through the ward, where all these crazy ladies were,
she became aware of her environment. They had to
take her to a padded cell and strap her down. She
went berserk, screaming and getting violent. Then,
we were told to leave. Her screams of terror followed
us all the way out. I kept thinking, "Dear God, what
have I done?" To my dying day, I will hear her cries.
They told us later that she tore up the place, for
such a little gal she had the strength of a lion. They
gave her a sedative so she could get some rest and
told us not to come back for a few days, to give her
time to adjust.

I called all the time. I asked the nurse to have
her call me collect if it were at all possible. Days went
by and finally, I got a call telling me I could come
and visit, and to bring some things Shirley needed.
They gave me a list over the phone, and my heart
was singing, my footsteps were lighter as I was going
to see my little girl. I kept thinking, is she going to
hate me?

My friend went with me and we did not know what to expect. Would Shirley be angry and not want to see me? We could only hope and pray that this would be a happy reunion. A nurse met us at the door of the hospital and took us to the area where Shirley was. She was chatting with other patients and when she noticed we were there she came over to us and gave me a big hug and kiss. My worries were all for naught. What a difference, she was a different little girl. She had been making little craft things for her boys and couldn't wait to show us. And she was anxious for me to deliver her gifts for her. She seemed to be her old self.

She loved her boys, but on the other hand I had the feeling she could not cope. How would she handle it when she came home and was by herself? She met a woman from Port Orchard and they hit it off real well. This little woman had a lot of imaginary phobias and she would talk about them and laugh about them. But, she would get real nervous and upset when she talked about her husband.

They were not in a locked ward and could come and go when they weren't in group. The cafeteria was the hang out for the younger patients and they would drink gallons of coffee. If they weren't smokers, they soon took up the habit. Shirley became a smoker—one habit to replace another. She was a patient for over a month. We felt she really didn't want to come home to face being a housewife and mother. It was the housewife part that seemed to get to her. She was happy to be with the boys, but she couldn't stand her life and started going around with the wrong people.

She wanted a divorce and her husband did not
contest it. One day, a cousin of Franks came to visit
and wanted to help. He offered to take Shirley to
Oregon where his family was involved in a religious
cult. He was sure they could help her. Shirley went
willingly and stayed with his family. They were so good
to her and wanted her to become a member. They
badgered her all the time, and she said she didn't
want to join that church because she considered
herself a Catholic.

One of her boys, Mark, was living with her, and
she left that religious group and got an apartment.
Her son was going to junior high and was involved in
sports. Shirley would go with him to all his games
sometimes even to practice. It was then that she met
a man who owned a taxi cab business. Shirley would
get a cab to go home. He would take them home,
and he never charged them anything. He was a little
bit older than she was and had lost his wife. He also
had two boys who were both out of school.

Elmer was such a kind and considerate man, he
knew that our girl was hurting. He told me she was
like an injured little kitten when he met her. He just
wanted to protect and take care of her. He asked
her to marry him and she said she would have to
think it over. She called me and told me what a kind
man he was and that she never had anyone treat her
so special. She worried about the age difference,
however. I told her age is all in the mind. If she cared
about him enough to make that commitment, then
she should go for it. So, they had a quiet wedding,
and when the boys were on spring break we all went
to visit them.

We liked Elmer immediately. He called Shirley

his little kitten. She fit right in with his taxi business. She could work in the office, take calls and relay them to him on his route and do the bookwork. He would call her from his cab phone to see if she was O.K. He knew about her addiction and would go out of his way to make sure she didn't get bored. He would get home about one o'clock every morning and if she was upset and lonesome for her other boys, he would take her out for a drive. She usually wanted to go to the ocean, to Lincoln City for crab and or shrimp. She did love her seafood. Not many men would be so thoughtful.

When Joseph and I would go to Oregon for an annual rock hunting trip we always stopped in to see Shirl and Elmer. We would take Shirl out for the day, as we usually had her boys with us and they liked to go rock hunting, digging and the whole bit. Shirley just enjoyed watching us all dig while she laid in the sun. We had a cabover camper and I enjoyed cooking up a big meal for all of us. One time I put a roast in the oven along with all the veggies. Oh, the aroma, it smelled so good! Every one in the camp site was sniffing the breeze. These good times I will always remember. This day I will always cherish.

Fall and winter fell upon us, and I began worrying about our girl. She went to the doctor, because she was having a lot of female problems. She was supposed to have an operation for what they said was a "pre-cancerous cervix" and she was back on drugs given to her by the doctors to help ease the pain. With Elmers help she only took the correct amount. The doctors wanted to operate, but Shirley wanted to wait for spring break after Easter.

She was planning a big week with all her boys. She called me to ask if I would be able to come and be with her when she had her surgery. "Oh, I forgot Mom," she said, "You are working and can't come." I said, "Honey, I will give up my job if I have to, you are more important than any job, you come first." She seemed so relieved.

On March 4th she called me and the boys and talked up a storm telling us how she couldn't wait for Easter, telling us she was baking pies and had Elmer buy the biggest turkey he could find. She asked if I had gotten the plant she had sent to me for my birthday. I said, "yes," and thanked her for being so thoughtful, She had to tell me how to take care of it. I assured her I would do my best to keep it alive. I really didn't have much luck with house plants. We chatted for a long time and she said she was tired and for me to tell Dad she loved him and said, "Mama, I love you too." We said our goodnights. I went to bed feeling loved, but also with a heavy heart.

My birthday came and the morning after, we were awakened by the ringing of the telephone. It was Elmer calling to tell us our first born had died. We were all in shock.

Elmer told us she was O.K. when he came home at one o'clock, and that he had stopped in about 11 o'clock to see how she was. She had just taken a shower, her hair was in rollers and she was all settled in to watch a good movie. She asked Elmer to be quiet when he came home as she was going right to bed after her movie was over.

Elmer said he came home at the usual time and peeked into see how she was. She seemed to be resting, so he took his shower and went to read the paper, but decided to look in on her again. She was laying flat on her back and seemed to be struggling for breath. She told him if she was flat on her back, for him to roll her over as she had a hard time breathing. Elmer very gently rolled her over, she gurgled and with one long sigh, she was gone. He called the medics and the ambulance came. They worked over her for an hour, Elmer would not let them give up. He was sure they could revive her. Finally at five o'clock a.m. he called us to tell us the sad news. It's not fair if you don't outlive your children. She carried a very heavy cross all her life. We can only trust in our Lord, as we were taught that it is all in His hands. I feel she had her hell on this earth.

We buried Shirley in Oregon. All her family was in Washington, and I wanted her home. Joseph and I made our annual trip to Oregon to rock hunt and we visited her grave site. Elmer moved and also retired, so we did not know where he was. We knew he was in the same area, but did not know where. During one of our visits I went into a phone booth to look him up. I found him, and we had a very pleasant chat on the phone. I was shaking like a leaf, but I had to ask him if we could have our girl moved home to Port Orchard. I told him we could all visit her and this is where she belonged. He told me he had bought two lots and he would have to sell them. He said he would think it over and let me know. I did not get the support I wanted from my family because they all thought it would be best if we left her there. Yes, they could make this rash decision, they did not give this child life, or carry her under their heart.

Only a mother knows the anguish of losing a child. Of course I have a lot of guilt—I should have done this, or done that. Elmer finally called and said yes, she could be moved, but he could not afford the cost. I went to our local mortuary to find out all the details and then I purchased three lots, so Joseph and I and our Shirley could be together.

I made all the arrangements, our Shirley was brought home the day before Memorial Day. She was home and I did not tell anyone. One day we went to a first communion mass for a niece, and I went to the priest and asked him if he would go to the cemetery and bless her grave. He said yes he would be happy to. After mass we were invited to brother Tonys for cake and ice cream to celebrate the first communion. I asked Tony and Fern if they would come with us to the cemetery. Only then did I tell them why. At this time I also told Joseph. Tony and Fern were real happy for us. Joseph was real pleased that I went ahead and followed the dictates of my heart. He said he thought we would have to have another funeral and he couldn't face that again.

I did not tell her boys but they heard she was home. Tom, her oldest, went searching for her grave. We only had a little marker, since I had ordered a bronze one but it took time to make. I placed a large bouquet of french lilacs on her grave and that is how Tom found her. "There are grandma's lilacs." It was dusk and he had to light matches to read her name. He had used up all his matches when he spotted the lilacs. He was so relieved and torn with emotion, that he lay prostrate on her grave and talked to her. His wife was worried because he did not come home for hours. This was the beginning of healing for Tom. He took his boys to her grave and they put flowers on it. This way the boys knew that this was their grandma. Her picture is displayed in their home and they are pleased to tell others about their grandma.

The other boys had their own methods of handling their grief. Their mama would be so pleased and happy if she could see all her grandchildren, and know that her sons all married lovely women.

I am sure to this day she is aware of all the happenings and is with them in spirit, guiding and loving them.

Shirley

Shirley's Sons: Left to Right Tony, Mark, Mary, Ron, Tom

Top: William John, Michael Anthony, Thomas James
Bottom: Patricia Joann, Christopher Raymond

BVG